THE
IGNORANT
MAESTRO

THE
IGNORANT
MAESTRO

How Great Leaders Inspire
Unpredictable Brilliance

ITAY TALGAM
with LARY BLOOM

PORTFOLIO / PENGUIN

PORTFOLIO / PENGUIN
Published by the Penguin Publishing Group
Penguin Random House LLC
375 Hudson Street
New York, New York 10014

USA | Canada | UK | Ireland | Australia | New Zealand | India | South Africa | China
penguin.com
A Penguin Random House Company

First published by Portfolio / Penguin, an imprint of Penguin Publishing Group, a
division of Penguin Random House LLC, 2015

ISBN 978-1-59184-723-6
ISBN 978-1-59184-812-7 (Export Edition)

Printed in the United States of America
1   3   5   7   9   10   8   6   4   2

Set in Bell MT
Designed by Spring Hoteling

The book is dedicated to my children: Imri, Assaf, and Alma. I am grateful to all three of them for teaching me so much, each in his or her own way, and for the unending joy they bring into my life.

CONTENTS

PART ONE | 1

The Music of Business

PART TWO | 17

Three New Themes of Leadership

    CHAPTER ONE | 19

    A Brilliant Ignorance

    CHAPTER TWO | 41

    Don't Mind the Gap

    CHAPTER THREE | 59

    Keynote Listening

CONTENTS

PART THREE | 73
Six Musical Variations on the Themes of Leadership

    CHAPTER FOUR | 83
    Command and Control: Riccardo Muti

    CHAPTER FIVE | 103
    The Godfather: Arturo Toscanini

    CHAPTER SIX | 119
    Play by the Book: Richard Strauss

    CHAPTER SEVEN | 137
    The Leader as Guru: Herbert von Karajan

    CHAPTER EIGHT | 157
    Leadership Dance: Carlos Kleiber

    CHAPTER NINE | 179
    In Search of Meaning: Leonard Bernstein

Optimistic Coda: What Now? | 211

Acknowledgments | 217

Notes | 221

THE
IGNORANT
MAESTRO

Part ONE

The Music of Business

The podium—my little orchestra conductor's office—is a space meant for just one person. But today I invite you to stand with me in that open-space cubicle as we study together the music of leadership.

Don't worry. It doesn't matter if your CV doesn't list perfect pitch, or if you're not sure of the difference between an oboe and an English horn. You won't need to bother, either, about the meaning of *glissando* or *rubato*. Nevertheless, you *will* get a unique vantage point for understanding why music making is an ideal metaphor for leadership that broadens individual opportunities as it enhances collective effort. Indeed, everything that happens on our podium sheds light on the most common and pressing issues faced by leaders, offering solutions in contexts that have nothing to do with Mozart or Stravinsky.

For twenty years, in addition to being a conductor of orchestras, I have been a conductor of people in business and other vital pursuits. I have used the lessons of the podium to advise leaders in fields I know next to nothing about, ranging from global political figures to start-up entrepreneurs, from scientific researchers to antiterrorist combat units, from advertising agencies to refugee agencies, in scales ranging from CEOs of Fortune 100 companies to parents and their kids. My teaching and learning during these two decades are at the heart of *The Ignorant Maestro*.

These lessons may lead us to some unexpected perspectives, where you begin to listen to the world around you, people and work included, in a musical way, identifying patterns within a flow. Ideas may arise that seem unsound—or even alarmingly stupid—for instance, as the book's title suggests, choosing ignorance. That might seem a terrible quality to exhibit in your workplace—a sure path down the stairs and out the corporate door. But stick with me here and see how it leads you upward—you'll understand why the greatest leaders not only embrace ignorance but are convinced it is an essential choice on their part, allowing their people to reach upper floors that haven't even been built yet.

Indeed, you'll need to be agile and flexible as we proceed. At times, our little podium will get more crowded, as we are joined by a few of the greatest conductors ever, such as my own mentor, the legendary Leonard Bernstein.

One thing all conductors, great and small, have in common: We all use the same musical aid that makes no sound and requires no expensive carrying case—a stick. Yet in some hands this silent and dead piece of wood, the baton, can be exceptionally potent. An old proverb says: "If you look at zero, you see zero. If you look *through* zero, you see infinity." Our baton is that zero, in itself of no use to an orchestra even if we wave it elegantly. Only when we are able to make our musicians look *through* the stick and see the full scope of artistic and human achievement embedded in the music—only then have we touched the true essence of the conductor's art. In fact, it is the essence of every leader's art, vital to all who conduct business and other high-stakes enterprises far beyond the walls of the concert hall.

On the following pages, you and I (and a few of the greatest conductors of the last hundred years) will be looking at this miracle of leadership taking place. We shall see how gaps of all kinds become a source of creative energy and new discoveries. We shall also transform ourselves from the accomplished keynote speakers that we are into keynote listeners, creating change with our ears only.

We will do that while conducting ourselves in places that never etched the word "music" into their mission statements—places such as Goldman Sachs, Merck, Kraft Foods, even in military headquarters on the Syrian border. These organizations represent a very large number of people—in all walks of professional life—who found inspiration in understanding the leadership of great conductors. I was there to see their fascination turn into insight.

Remember, you don't need to be a lover of classical music to understand this. Because music is everywhere, and you already know a great deal about it—only, most probably, you do not think of your everyday reality in musical terms. But that is about to change.

We are all musical creatures, immersed in sound. I'm not referring to elevator music, the radio, or the songs collected in your iTunes library. What I refer to here is the consistent process of making sense out of the sound around you. These sounds are the first ones to notice as you consider the measures necessary to become a better leader.

Let's say, for example, that you take the commuter

train to work. The repetitive sound of the train moving along the tracks sings to you, reassures you. Although you may not be aware of why you feel a certain sense of calm and well-being, it is thanks to that rhythmic evidence that you are nearing your destination.

And let's say that at the end of that train ride you hail a taxi. Elements of music appear in the cab's sudden starts and stops, in the nervous changing of lanes, in the driver screaming at other drivers. This is music noisy and chaotic, so your nervous system reacts: It drives you crazy. If, on the other hand, you are lucky enough to ride your bike to the office, you become part of a different, calmer music; there is a natural alignment between the way you move your body and the speed you are going, in correlation with the changes of light and terrain. This movement harmonizes you.

When you finally arrive at work, what kind of music surrounds you? Walk around and listen, then ask yourself: Where is the beat coming from? That is, where would you look if you wanted to see what kind of day lies ahead for the business—the mailroom? R&D? HR? Is there a conductor, someone everyone looks toward? It could be the CEO, but maybe not. Maybe it's someone lower in the chain. Does the music empower you, or make you feel helpless? Are you distracted by loud sounds, by some out-of-tune horns? If you want to concentrate, must you put in earplugs and close yourself off in your workspace, or do you have the urge to join the chorus and celebrate the collective efforts of colleagues? While attending a meeting, do you hear a love duet, or a fatal scene from a tragic opera? And how about your own part in the music making of your workplace? Is it audible at all? Do you ever get to play the lead role—the beautiful melodies—or just the old um-cha-cha? And how is your music perceived from the outside? Are the neighbors complaining? Is your audience of customers happy? And most important—could all of that be different?

You sit at your desk on a Monday morning. Everything seems normal for the start of the workweek, except that a light flickers above you. This distracts you for a moment, but then you remember you must find an important document for a client. You open your desk drawer to fetch it. And when you look up, you can't believe what you don't see.

Your computer is missing. Your desk is gone, too, as are the bookshelf and credenza. Indeed, the whole office has vanished. In front of you, instead of a nameplate that says "Senior Investment Manager" there is a music stand. The document doesn't list quarterly revenues. It says, Mozart: *Eine Kleine Nachtmusik*. And then you hear people around you tuning instruments. You realize you are unaccountably sitting in the back of the second violin section of a symphony orchestra, violin in hand, just as rehearsal is about to begin. How could this be?

But soon your confusion turns to elation. After all, you've always enjoyed music, and though you've never taken a violin lesson in your life, now you can apparently play like a real pro while your colleagues back in the office keep up the numbers, calm nervous investors, and moan about the firm's lack of professional opportunity. How lucky you are. If only Schwartz from Accounting, that perpetual annoyance, could see you now.

But wait a minute. Isn't that Schwartz from Accounting sitting in the first violin section, closer to the conductor? Schwartz? How did that happen? Anyway, no time for pondering now: The maestro gives a sign and the music starts. You play like a demon, determined to outshine that good-for-nothing from Accounting. Can't they see he's an impostor? Surely the conductor will notice your efforts instead. And he does.

He stares you down, and says in a harsh tone, "What are you doing? You're supposed to be playing with the others. I want all the second violins to sound like one instrument. I don't want sixteen egomaniacs demanding attention." You, of course, are crushed. And you look over at Schwartz from Accounting. He's beaming.

Later, backstage on break, you realize the insult to you

is of no interest to your new colleagues. Fellow violinists are busy complaining about how hard they work compared to others in the orchestra. "Too many notes to play," says one. Another mentions the triangle player. "He plays his 'ping' once every half hour and he gets more money than we do. Some 'soloist' he is." You overhear a clarinetist and oboist in conversation. The clarinetist says, "I'm sick and tired of the strings always playing out of tune. If I hear them for four hours a day, I'm going to lose my own precious sense of tuning." The oboist nods, and says, "For years I haven't listened to them at all." Then a trumpet player joins the complaint fest. "How long are we going to put up with this idiot conductor? The only way for us to play together is to ignore him completely."

The bell signaling the end of the break rings loudly. But this bell turns out to be the telephone on your office desk. The music stand with the Mozart is gone and your old computer screen resurfaces with the latest profit and loss figures displayed. Schwartz from Accounting is still in the office closer to the boss. What a sycophant. In short order, you are back in the old mess. And you wonder: Is everywhere the same? Could it be that the Pursuit of Aggravation is a mission statement in every organization, from investment banks to academic institutions to symphony orchestras?

Your soul, however, rebels against such pessimism. Surely people can be happy and fulfilled in their work. It's not impossible, is it? When each morning you leave home, kiss your spouse and children good-bye, are you obliged to leave your heart there as well? Or can the workplace be a spiritual place, an expression of life as you want to live it? Of course it can, you assure yourself. The answer is as clear as the sound of the overpaid triangle player. It is not to be found in a shining profit and loss statement, not even in Mozart's masterpieces, but rather in the music of our work life, music we produce and experience with others around us.

So let's say you could have your way and could change the metaphorical music of the workplace any way you like. That is, you can give prominence to the kind of flow that you believe would move your collective effort to the next level. You can set the pace and make sure that there is enough structure to sustain the flow. You can instill space for individual expression into the music, if you believe this is needed, and determine the kind of give-and-take among players. You can create predictability or strive for surprise. In short, it's your call: You are the designer of your organization, the composer and the orchestrator of its flow of work.

Your first tendency might be to put on the music you

like to relax with—that would be nice, surely. But wait a minute—would it fit? After all, we're not just about everybody chilling out together. You want work to be done.

Music has at times had the desired influence on you and people around you. It stirred you, energized you, and made you collaborate with other people easily and harmoniously. What was it? What music can stir the heart, help harmonize and inspire change and innovation, and bring people together? If you were the best leader you could be, what kind of music would come to mind for people taking part in your organization?

Perhaps a marching band playing Sousa's "The Stars and Stripes Forever." Yes! Everyone in step with the beat of the drums and cymbals. This music is so full of optimism and forward movement. People in the organization have no choice but to listen and to be in perfect alignment along a straight road. You can see your clients on the sidewalk, cheering, waving little flags bearing your company's logo. But wait, what if you have to stop and think for a minute? You can't, because the big drum never stops. What if the drum major takes the band in the wrong direction, as in the film *Animal House*, when one row after another of blind followers marches into a brick wall? So no, it can't really be a marching band, can it? Not enough flexibility. Maybe there's another, more subtle, metaphorical solution. How about celestial harmony?

As you sit in the cathedral, glowing light comes from stained glass windows high above. Everywhere you look are beauty and dignity. The choir sings ancient church music in perfect harmony, led by an expressive conductor who seems to lift the singers toward heaven. My God, you think (literally). If only it could be this way with marketing and sales. A lower voice supports the others, enabling them, and you think, ah, the reliable IT department. And so you paint this ideal picture of what a workplace can be. But you then realize for the last hour you have lost all sense of time and connection with the outer world. With this beauty, centuries can pass and the world can turn upside down but the music is the same music. It is time-less, yes, but dangerous if you want to be relevant and innovative. It has very little to do with the fast-changing circumstances of society. True, you'd like to hear workers in perfect harmony. But there is a labor churn, people come and go, and they are reluctant to get in the constraints of your company's harmonization, and HR hasn't the time to train all the new people, anyhow. So the perfect harmony dissipates. You need another solution. Something upbeat? Dixieland jazz?

Now you turn your company into a version of Pres-ervation Hall in New Orleans. And, as the saints go marching in, smiles on their faces, all the people play-ing independent melody lines, improvising off the top of their heads, it somehow works together. They make you tap your toes and snap your fingers. Customers know the tune, so they maintain a feeling of safety even when improvisation gets wild. Who wouldn't want music, work, and life itself to be a Dixieland jazz band? The trouble is that in the end, the group comes back to the same theme over and over again. For as innovative and creative as it all is, it's also repetitive, and though it has a happy ending, it all ends there. There is no chance for it to morph into something else or incorporate a different mood. Your customers are less satisfied after a while, no longer enchanted by a charm that's worn off. The innovation is on one level only, on the surface, because the structure never changes. Well, then, perhaps you haven't been bold enough, staying within your own cultural safety zone. Maybe you should go off the musical deep end. Maybe take the Orient Express heading east?

Middle Eastern music usually features one solid stream of sound, with everyone in the band playing and singing the same melody, or seemingly so. When you get closer, when you really listen, you hear something unexpected. Each of the participants has a different version of the melody. You open the door to one office, and you listen to what the guy is doing there. He's playing little trills to embellish the melody, ornaments that make the music richer. The woman in the other office sings higher, and her version is leaner. Though there is one big wave of sound, there are a lot of variations to the individual parts. There's a feeling of togetherness, yet a sense of individual creativity. Isn't that the atmosphere you want at the office? Customers hear a clear melody, not something chaotic, and can still find variety to suit personal taste. But this, too, has its limits. You go to your bank branch to apply for a loan. The manager says all the right things but she won't give you the money. So you go to a different loan officer at the same bank who looks at the same material and she says she can do it. Why different answers? Because this bank's rules are like Middle Eastern music—they allow for this lack of precision. Middle Eastern music scales have more notes than the Western scales, notes that are somewhere between tones and microtones, that are all over the place, creating endless, beautiful micro-complications. They are saying yes and no and maybe at the same time. Ambiguity creates great moments, but it is frustrating as a system with long-range direction. Where is the consistency? Where is the reliability? So this music obviously has its limits for your business. Shall we try another genre? Remember your last visit to the symphony? Call it the Classic Solution?

This is the old standby. In a Beethoven symphony, you have large-scale architecture. This enables extended exploration of ideas, creating a sense of permanence and power. It doesn't make you dance at any given moment—your analytical side is often called to work. The techniques used in symphonic writing connect the short and the long term through a process of continuous development. Symphonic music calls for intensive interaction between orchestral sections. Percussion and horns are very different from strings, but they are all aware of, depend on, and support each other. And so the expectations are that with all musicians working together, your company will get fantastic results about, say, four years from now. It will be everything you hoped for in the way of returns. The only problem is that the whole industry may shift in a few months. Think of eight-track tapes: great, but obsolete. Think Kodak film, gone. Think typewriters, on which so many great works of literature were created, out. In all of your finery and with all of your depth, you may not be nimble enough to respond. You might be building a great idea for the automotive industry, but oil prices go up in four years and you become completely irrelevant. This work is only about the long term and, as such, is destined to create long-term problems. Not a perfect solution, regrettably—at least not for everyone.

Is there a one-size-fits-all solution to suit all kinds of organizations in every stage of their lives? It is most unlikely. Even if an organization does find its perfect solution, chances are it will have to be modified or changed when the world renders it irrelevant. As leaders we have to learn how to change from one form of music to another, and take the whole organization with us. We might have to learn how to combine different models, different musical forms, to create something new and vital. What do leaders need to be in order to go beyond their comfort zone and become more effective in an ever-changing world?

The self-exploration we propose here will not be easy. It requires full attention and a level of openness that doesn't come naturally to many in positions of authority. But by now I hope you see music not only as an art form or even an attractive metaphor, but also as a lens and a language for observing and discussing issues of organization. And that you are willing to provide for yourself a kind of leadership iTunes collection, one that, as the pages in this book are turned, will become refined to your particular needs and personality, a unique creation of your own set of leadership ears.

Part
TWO

Three New Themes of Leadership

Ignorance, Gaps, and Keynote Listening:
Three "Negatives" with the Most Positive Outcomes

If you look at your knowledge, your skills, your experience—in short, at the entire inventory of assets you put on your CV—you see only half of your value proposal, an essential half, for which you must have worked hard. The other half is just as important, but you never put it on your résumé. You may write: "I will bring knowledge to the team," but you never write: "I will bring ignorance, and I relentlessly encourage my team to go beyond my knowledge to a higher place." You may write: "I am good at bringing people together and in unifying procedures." You never write: "I am good at identifying gaps in the organization, and making sure they are exposed so we can all benefit from them." You may write: "I excel in communicating my decisions so that they are clear," but you never write: "I prefer to listen to my team rather than instruct them; my listening brings success to the team."

As you are beginning to sense, all three elements mentioned above are connected. They all contain spaces of special dynamic qualities. Ignorance is coupled with a will to explore new space, gaps contain hidden potential waiting to be uncovered, and "keynote listening"—that is, listening that can change views and agendas—can make use of space to allow other people to fully express themselves in dialogue.

Your willingness to let go of your knowledge and embrace ignorance will be the crucial tipping point in adopting your new leadership assets. In order to take that leap, you will have to feel confident as a leader both in your task of gap exploration and in your growing skill of keynote listening.

CHAPTER ONE

A Brilliant Ignorance

A new and promising sense of ignorance has emerged for me, a process that began about two decades ago. It resulted in the understanding that the creation of new, unpredictable knowledge is to be achieved by combining existing knowledge, will, and finally, *the conscious decision to be ignorant,* to not know the answers, not even to try to predict them. The story below reveals how I came upon this idea. You will note that gaps play a crucial role in the story of how I learned to appreciate my ignorance.

In the summer of 1996, I built sand castles on the

beach in Tel Aviv with my two young boys, feeling as if the school break would last forever and that the cultural season was blessedly still far away. My state of summertime easy living, however, was interrupted by a phone call of a peculiar nature.

My friend Yuval Ben-Ozer, a conductor of choral ensembles, explained that he had been asked by the head of human resources of a national bank to talk to senior managers about classical music. This seemed odd to Yuval. Especially because the HR director pointed out that these managers had no interest at all in classical music. Why then, Yuval had asked her, inflict this idea on them? She replied that a little bit of culture might be helpful, though she wasn't sure exactly how.

I was glad when Yuval asked me to do the presentation with him. But how could we create some sort of tangible value for this particular audience? I couldn't help thinking of the intimidating gaps between us musicians and the big-shot bankers. I envisioned myself riding to the presentation on my rusted bike, while their Mercedes 500s filled up the parking lot. There was, for me, a threatening gap there. Then I sensed a gap of a different nature; thinking of it now, I admit, doesn't make me proud. I had a vague feeling of cultural superiority, as if I knew that however talented those financial wizards were in their narrow materialistic game, they could never match me, the Artist, on that score. I clung to this advantage to compensate for my miserable shortcomings on financial matters.

Yet the issue of my ignorance concerning the nature of their jobs confounded me. I couldn't imagine what it felt like to be responsible for investments of billions, or for downsizing a large organization and sending thousands of employees to the insecurity of unemployment. I considered my options of creating a foothold for myself in their world: Should I try reading up on the banks' system? Change my political (and moral) views of capitalism? Finally and most important, what could I teach them, considering their lack of interest in music? They were older than I and they were infinitely more experienced in managing people on a large scale. The bank's tens of thousands of employees made my seventy-six-player-strong Tel Aviv Symphony Orchestra seem irrelevant. What precious ideas could I bring to them that they didn't know already?

I had no answers, but I had passion about music to share, and in at least one sense I was playing from strength because classical music is reputed to be something serious and respectable. The special aura of "the maestro" (although I never felt I deserved this title) might buy me a few minutes of curious attention. But not more than a few. I had to hook the execs and keep them hooked.

Here's what I settled on: Instead of telling them, I would show them. Instead of fearing my ignorance and theirs and my complicated relation to rich people and theirs to "artist" types and all the gaps between us, I would just put something beautiful in front of us all. Then I could just listen to them, and, perhaps, a fruitful discussion would result. It had to be something I was passionate about, and it had to be something they could relate to without my telling them what to look for: Yes, conductors! Leaders and managers, with 100 percent visibility. All they would have to do is watch.

I turned to my video library and looked for those moments in conducting that were burned in my memory as extraordinary, holding the essence of what great conducting means. It took me no more than a couple of hours to locate short clips of half a dozen great conductors in concert performances. I showed the clips to Yuval, and we tried to interpret the work of these conductors not in musical terms but from the position of leadership. What kind of leaders were they? And what could we all learn from them? Once we settled on this idea, we felt ready to go.

There were about thirty people in the conference room, chairs arranged in an intimate semicircle, like a small orchestra. The HR executive provided an introduction in which she said only, "The two guest speakers come from another world, and their knowledge is encoded in a different language, but I know they have something to show that will be helpful to us."

And off we went. I said, "Remember the last time you came into a music venue and took your seat, a few minutes before the start of the show? You watched the players on-stage as they played little riffs on their own instruments, unrelated, and without regard to what the person on the right or left played. This created a chaotic cloud of disso-nant sounds." Since everyone at one time or another had heard some sort of live music onstage, tuning into that memory was easy. "But what about your professional life—any such chaotic behaviors?"

"All the time!" came a cheerful cry.

"And what happens next onstage?" I said. "They are tuning. One player stands up and plays one note—the 'stan-dard'—and everyone makes a public commitment to play-ing that one note in exactly the same way. Any parallels from the office?"

"Well, of course," came a reply, "we have a lot of rules we're all supposed to go by. But I'm not sure we all do . . ."

The connection lies in the dual nature of playing in an orchestra. On the one hand, it's all about you as an in-dividual musician. You undertake your warm-up rituals without regard to anyone else on the stage, because in a very transparent organization you are fully accountable for your playing, and you want to perform well. But then in very short order it also becomes necessary to be totally committed to a certain standard for the group. So there is a tense balance between the solo playing and the need for collaboration—exactly the same balance that businesses face when they want to encourage individual excellence and team playing at the very same time.

While I briefly mentioned the conductor, facing the daunting challenge of coordinating dozens of sensitive artists, all with fairly considerable egos, I could see curiosity on the faces of our bankers, and hear an amused chatter: They knew something about ego too.

I could relax now. The gaps between us were still there, but these gaps didn't define us anymore. There were deeper notions of human behavior that could provide us with an observation frame we could share, so we could explore the gaps, each of us using an individual language to describe what we see.

To begin, I looked for a musical example of the elusive phenomenon of harmony, in a broad sense. Never to be taken lightly, in small organizations (marriage comes to mind!) or large ones, harmony for me is far from a state of Nirvana, a final, eternal, unchanging state of bliss. Harmony, in music and in life itself (including business life), is rather a continuous flow of well-coordinated movements and evolving relations between all who take part—sometimes dissonant relations, resolving in a higher state of agreement—creating a sense of achievement and joy.

So we all watched the Vienna Philharmonic in a New Year's Day concert playing its traditional closing, "The Radetzky March." My seminar participants observed a dancing, joyful conductor. They heard superb playing by every instrumentalist, and they saw each of the 2,000 people in the Vienna concert hall, a normally very conservative and reserved place, joining in by clapping to the rhythm of the music. As clapping is contagious, some in the conference room started doing it themselves. There was a sense of harmony that we were somehow part of—I knew that because everyone in the room was smiling.

"Would you call this a success?" asked Yuval.

A resounding "Yes!" came from the group.

"So whom would you like to congratulate for this achievement of harmony?"

What followed was unexpected: Everyone had something to say. We heard many statements that began "I don't know much about classical music." Then, defying what they just said, many launched into observations and analyses of how the whole thing works, in which they could identify the contributions of specific individuals to the success, including the composer and even the clapping audience. I said, "These people understand and engage so well in the 'product' that they want to become, symbolically, part of the orchestra and the music making. Isn't that the kind of relations you would like with your customers? That they know exactly when to listen carefully to you, the professionals, when they need to back you up, clapping to your rhythm? And even to have them so grateful that when you come to the office in the morning your clients are waiting at the door, clapping as you enter?"

Smiles again: The need for recognition is universal, and again it seems that our common human needs are mirrored in everything we do. Inherently we all know that, but somehow, in the process of becoming experts and specialists, we narrow our interests and forget it, until we are reminded. These moments of awareness of some knowledge waiting to emerge reminded me of the old story the rabbis tell, that infants in the womb know the Torah by heart but when they are born an angel taps them on the head, making them forget, and they spend the rest of their lives rediscovering what they already know.

As the seminar participants discovered the validity of their observations, the divisions between us seemed less like obstacles, more like a way to gain new perspective. There was no hierarchy now between our different disciplines, but an exchange of ideas that could be discussed and valued by all, based on their content, rather than on who owned them.

At this point I proposed to play a game, after the format of *American Idol*. The idea was to appoint all the participants as jurors and bring a line of candidates for their consideration. I asked the executives at the meeting to choose which one of the conductors they would like to see working with them as senior managers, leaders of the bank.

Our audience had no prior knowledge of my candidates, and this ignorance was liberating; they could use what they saw as a trigger for free association. We watched together in silence at first, but the quiet didn't last. There was clapping in the room, there was laughter; there were remarks that showed they could connect what they saw on the screen with their everyday existence in their mahogany offices. "Remember old Berkowitz in investments? Exactly this guy." And, "Did you see that look he gave them? Chilling! Someone will be looking for a new job."

Obviously, having to vote made our game partners more invested in the conversation—a game is a serious thing, after all. This game provided a safe space in being remote enough from the everyday workplace, reality, and it also provided an extra safety net: They couldn't make a wrong choice; these were all great conductors. So my participants could afford to take risks, to explore and fail, and have fun doing so. On the other hand, the very fact that they could play the game—that they could develop strong arguments for and against candidates—proved the game's relevancy to themselves and their work.

Soon the discussion gravitated toward themselves: their attitudes, values, priorities, likes and dislikes. They were still asking and commenting about the different conductors. There was great, visible diversity to absorb and interpret: What does dancing have in common with conducting? How different is the sound in response to short, angular hand movements, as opposed to round movements of the arms? But their interpretations and applications to their own work emerged in parallel. The two lines converged in a funny way when one of them interrupted another, and he was admonished by the first speaker, "Let me finish—don't conduct me like that dictator in the video!"

The session in Tel Aviv went on for longer than planned, and as we left, the room was buzzing with conversation, ideas, smiles. We felt we'd done something right, hitting a rich vein, but with what tool did we open it? If we could identify it, we could hope to replicate our success.

I had to wait about fifteen years, until my son Imri, by then a concert pianist with a keen interest in philosophy, introduced me to a text that solved the riddle of what had become my new professional life.

It turned out that I was fulfilling the greatly satisfying role of an "ignorant teacher" without ever fully realizing it. Let me explain.

A French philosopher living today, Jacques Rancière, writes in *The Ignorant Schoolmaster* about the eccentric theory of a nineteenth-century French professor, Joseph Jacotot, who made this outrageous claim:

> An ignorant can teach another ignorant what
> he does not know himself.

This sentence, I find, needs to be read at least twice, and then (in my case, at least) it brings about a sense of disbelief mixed with wonder and joy. Is this possible? If true, it is as fantastic a discovery as the invention of a perpetual motion device. Each one of us can teach everyone else everything! In "ordinary" teaching one expects the teacher to know the subject matter—and clearly for every one thing we know we are ignorant of so many! Here, then, is a way of acquiring infinite new knowledge.

But how? How can illiterate parents teach reading to their children? We need to understand, says Jacotot, that being ignorant has nothing to do with being stupid. Moreover, basic to Jacotot's thinking is the claim of "the equality of intelligences," implying that the intelligence of an illiterate farmer, who is nevertheless knowledgeable about everything to do with the best way to grow crops, equals the intelligence of a good lawyer or a good scientist. Not only is their intelligence equal, but knowing one thing is like knowing another, in the sense that knowing this one thing is proof of your ability to learn others (Jacotot thought that learning your mother's tongue was proof enough!). So the teacher is only ignorant in the specific context of what he teaches. Moreover, the good teacher, even if he possesses the "relevant" knowledge, knows how to dissociate himself from that knowledge: He does not teach his knowledge to his students.

So what does the teacher do, and how can he become a masterful teacher? In Rancière's rather festive words, "He commands them [the students] to venture forth in the forest, to tell what they see, what they think of what they have seen." In other words, he encourages them to give their own interpretation of their discoveries. The teacher's challenge is to help the student whenever his power of will—not his intelligence—is failing him, facing the hardships of his study. He has to make sure the student pays attention. In doing this, the teacher verifies the learning process rather than its outcomes. The ignorant schoolmaster is "willfully ignorant" of the student's final learning concerning a certain phenomenon. His mastery is in helping the student discover something that he, the teacher, may be ignorant of himself.

As we turn our thoughts from teaching to leading, I believe Jacotot's radical view of the teacher's role translates into an equally radical and promising view of the leader's role. Our first step would be to embrace the idea that just as anyone can learn and teach, so is everyone a follower and a leader. "Leadership" is not an exclusive category of human behavior inaccessible to "followers."

The next step would be to understand the place of knowledge—this intellectual asset we all work so hard to acquire—in the making of a leader. What about our valuable hard-earned experience? Expertise? Are we now being asked to forget it and succumb to ignorance?

Again, the ignorance we preach is not of the classic definition, which may manifest itself in denying the danger of smoking or being unable to point to Nebraska on a map of the United States. We do obviously want leaders to be well informed and knowledgeable in their field of operation; people of broad understanding of the past and present state of their disciplines, and even have a wide knowledge in other fields. Knowledge of all types is needed in order to point in the direction of the "forest" (to use Rancière's image) to be explored. Our professional and political leaders do not need to forget what they know; they only need to dissociate themselves from their knowledge when "the search has begun," in other words, as they step into the future. They should be ready to leap into the unknown while not relying on their knowledge, without even predicting the outcome of the search. By making predictions, one can ruin the chance of discovering new knowledge.

How would knowledge and self-imposed ignorance work to create something utterly new? Let's consider one of the great innovators of all time: Ludwig van Beethoven. In what sense can one refer to Beethoven as '"ignorant" when writing a symphony? Surely he had to be extremely knowledgeable to compose a symphony—for example, he had to understand the technical possibilities of every instrument in the orchestra. He had to have extensive knowledge of the technique of writing music in the contemporary classical style, and in the older techniques—that was a necessary part of every composer's training: learning to speak "the language." What sets Beethoven apart from other composers is not superior knowledge of these and many other essential practices, but his ability to go beyond that knowledge, so his outcomes were unpredictable, to the point of surprising himself. He did that in spite of the reactions of the music professionals ("Obviously he is ripe for the madhouse" is a remark from a fellow composer). While certainly having a vision when setting to work, Beethoven was nevertheless searching the unknown, not knowing where he was going. He was experimenting, writing, and rewriting many times, until the work seemed finished.

The finished Beethoven manuscript is in itself a call for detailed study on the part of the musician performing it, as it is a call for ignorance. The standard way of writing music is not capable of denoting every aspect of the music in full precision, meaning that the musical text stays inherently open to different interpretations by the performers. The writing uses vague and relative terms—like *loud* and *soft*, or *fast* and *slow*—thus asking the knowledgeable yet creative performer to operate beyond the zone of definite knowledge. The sound actually produced—what we hear as music—will always contain an element of surprise, undetermined by the composer.

If we believe leaders—in every field—should provide their organizations with great plans, as great as Beethoven's symphonies, we should expect them to create their plans based on informed choices. At the same time, we should not want these plans to take a view of the future as solely determined by the past. There are, of course, lessons to be learned from the past, but these lessons may be too easily accepted and applied in a time when dynamics, business conditions, or the abilities of present-day personnel do not mirror the past. We want them to enable a difference from the past by being open to the unpredictable. In other words, we need them to choose ignorance, so that the future can be a matter of choice (with our having a say), rather than the outcome of inertial thinking.

Here is a leader in his field who embodies ignorance and knowledge in equal parts. My mentor in business ignorance, Yossi Vardi, is widely regarded as the guru of the Israeli high-tech industry. He made a considerable fortune by selling (with three bright younger inventors) a company called ICQ, which made pioneering instant messaging software, to AOL for $400 million in 1998.

This freed him to devote time to two parallel interests, both of them "ignorance based" in some sense. The first is investing in high-tech companies. Yossi has become what they call an "angel" investor in start-ups. He says his reason to invest in a start-up company is never that he thinks its product is bound be a success, simply because there is no way to predict success. In other words, Yossi admits to being ignorant of the success probability when making the investment. How, then, does he choose his companies? He does it by assessing the quality of the people. If they are good people—driven, innovative, trustworthy, determined, wise—then when they (most probably) fail, he can trust them to turn their initial failed idea in another direction until they get it right.

The other channel of Yossi's taste for ignorance is a series of events in the framework of "unconferences"— a term originally associated with Tim O'Reilly's Foo Camp.

Yossi started his line of unconferences with Kinnernet in Israel, and now its success is copied in different variations around the world. In Kinnernet, his flagship event, Yossi brings together about three hundred international entrepreneurs, inventors, artists, musicians, scientists, and other creative people to a conference that has no agenda or predetermined content at all (and pretty basic living conditions). The idea is that the participants will create the content: bring up ideas for discussions, organize musical events, create projects of technology, and so forth—including cooking some comparatively extravagant meals. The only tools supplied for the self-organizing event are big white boards on which the participants can freely add a session they wish to produce and try to get people to participate in it. These gatherings have very minimal structure and no top-down control— and they work. Issues of real interest to the participants are discussed, a wide range of perspectives is heard, new collaborations are formed, and new initiatives are born out of these unconferences, to be carried out in the real world. Sure enough, neither Yossi nor any of the other volunteers preparing the logistics for such camps are able to predict the outcomes. They are smart enough not even to try, and happily choose to embrace ignorance. In leadership terms, it means that at a certain point Yossi is willing to let go of control altogether—but not before he has created a very solid structure, a platform for this ignorance to work its magic. Apart from the essential logistics, there are strict rules of conduct for the participants: no business in camp, no criticism of other people's contributions ("Clap, even if you think what you heard is idiotic!"), no "drinking of other people's oxygen" (time is limited and everyone wants to participate), as Yossi puts it. By being uncompromising about those rules, the camp becomes a haven of goodwill, an environment temporarily free from selfishness. It is important to note that ignorance needs structure, rules, and careful listening to produce its outcomes.

In recent years I have tried to form a model for my own teaching, enabling me to summon ignorance within a structure, but I remember vividly how ignorance first caught me by surprise, and showed me that the unexpected was a goal, even when I thought I knew what I was doing.

It was in a seminar attended by spiritual leaders, somewhere near Atlanta, Georgia, in the late nineties. The people I met there were all very mindful of their communication skills, were focused on connecting, and were good listeners. And they sang together beautifully.

One evening, as they were about to resume singing, it suddenly dawned on me, being inspired by the group's passion, that there could be yet another mode to connect through singing. I was ignorant of what that something might be, but I felt led forward by the energy of the group. "Such beautiful singing," I said, "Can you walk around the room, singing and listening to other people?" They did, and a whole new dimension opened: It was like a still photo turning into a movie. The room sounded like a great kaleidoscope. I noticed that the beauty of the changing sound made people act as if they were inside their own private bubbles, enjoying the beautiful play of light on the surface. That made me say, "Please meet and acknowledge other people: Stand for a moment in front of a person, look at each other as you sing, shake hands before you move on."

As this started to happen, we were all experiencing something utterly new: having intimate bonding moments within the continuous reality of beautiful group harmony. Yet my personal moment of discovery was yet to come. I was excited and grateful for what took place, and so I said, "That was marvelous. Thank you!" in a concluding manner. I heard shushing sounds, and two hundred people were looking at me as if to say, "We don't want to stop."

They kept going another half an hour. It was time for me to let go of my control. We had created something together, something new that was enabled by our previous singing experiences, but could not have happened without our willingness to look for and experience something unknown. My choice to ask for something while having no idea where it might lead was an act of ignorant leadership, but so was the choice of the singing participants. So much so that they could overrule my wish to stop, having a better understanding than I did of the value of what was taking place.

Choosing ignorance as a positive line of action is not the result of fatigue, despair, or laziness in carrying out the search for relevant information. This choice is rather the result of understanding that comprehensive knowledge and previous experiences are essential in creating a platform on which ignorance can play its role. In our singing, it took a lot of individual skill and knowledge and group practice to get us singing together so well: That was the platform, plus the essential will not to stop there. To go further, we needed to become ignorant: Ignorance alone enables unpredictable learning and achievement.

What in the making of a platform might enable the moment of letting go on behalf of the leader? How does the right moment to assume ignorance present itself, and what should the leader be doing then? These are questions we shall be trying to answer in the chapters to follow. In the Six Musical Variations on the Themes of Leadership chapters, we will observe the degrees and various ways in which ignorance as a leadership tool is manifested in the work of great conductors.

CHAPTER TWO

Don't Mind the Gap

My own knowledge of gap handling comes from music. In fact, the essence of making music is in the treatment of gaps: the delight of gaps, the interpretation of gaps, using gaps to advantage. Quoting from Artur Schnabel, one of the greatest twentieth-century pianists: "The notes I can handle no better than many other pianists, but the pauses between the notes—ah, that's where the art resides."

Pauses can be perceived as voids—where nothing happens—or as gaps that give context and meaning to sounds. Indeed, the challenge of leadership in business, as in music, is to transform meaningless voids into meaningful gaps. Voids are defined negatively, as something missing, something that should have happened but didn't, so that people feel powerless about it: "Management never gives us answers—they are lost themselves," or "There are not enough resources allocated for customer support— we're gonna lose our customers and our jobs."

Gaps, on the other hand, are experienced as well-defined spaces, inviting exploration and creative work: "Management never tells us what to do; they expect us to propose the next steps, and bring them to the weekly open-content meeting," or "Not enough resources are allocated for customer support. Luckily, one of the guys in our team shared a link to a 'crowdsourcing' lecture he watched on TED talks; we're building a better model of support now— it will cost less and work better."

So what are gaps, and how are they recognized? Gaps occur to us as a sense of incompatibility: Something doesn't fit. They can appear in our perceptions, expectations, desires, visions, and in the way we communicate all those things.

Difference in itself does not constitute a gap: We can have two different visions, but a gap emerges only when we try to apply them both to the same reality— and they prove incompatible. A gap in communication may arise when the same text—a plan for a project—is interpreted differently by two people who try to work in cooperation.

A gap will occur when something taken for granted proves not to be the case. In other words, the coherence of one's worldview is compromised. Or it occurs when the narrative we tell ourselves about a certain aspect of our lives clashes with reality—when we think something doesn't make sense, or is funny and strange. Even funny that makes you laugh often builds on a sense of incompatibility.

Our Aversion to Gaps

Strong emotions—love, desire, loss, or even strong ambition—all these bring with them an acute sense of gap, which has to be dealt with. The deeper the gap is felt, the more energy it can create. Lovers will go to great lengths to get closer to their loved ones, as will ambitious entrepreneurs to attain success.

It seems that to experience a gap between yourself and someone (or something), you have to be, in one way or another, interested in that someone. If you are not interested, there is no gap.

This interest that we have in gaps projects toward the

future, to our intentions—what are we going to do about it? It seems that gaps, once perceived, call us to take action.

Now, all of the above sounds like, well, a nuisance. It seems that gaps signify mostly something wrong, a discrepancy. Why would anyone like gaps?

I would guess that your training and experience have taught you to avoid gaps. "Mind the Gap" as you walk out of a London tube train is an essential warning—the gap between the stopping train and the platform is a hazard, and it would be best if it did not exist at all. We can think of any number of physical, temporal, or perceptual gaps. Red lights when driving late to work—annoying! Gaps between election promises and action taken while in office— unfair! Gaps between what we ordered from the menu and what the waiter brought to our table—irritating! These gaps should not have been there in the first place. They should be eliminated, closed, cemented, sealed.

It seems, then, that the world would be a better place without gaps. But would it? Let's eliminate some every-day gaps. Just for fun. How about people getting from any place to any other in a split second—as in "Beam me up, Scotty!" on *Star Trek*—no need to waste time on the way? Tempting, isn't it? But what about the time it takes to switch your mind from, say, office mode to home mode? Or stopping on the way for a short espresso, watching people go by, not thinking—at least not being aware of thinking—for a few moments? Give it up? And when on vacation, would you be happy to find your boss beaming up to you for just a short question?

How would you like walking into a Van Gogh exhibition in which all the paintings had recently been "upgraded" so the gaps between the painter's view of the landscape and the "real" view we know from everyday experience has been eliminated? Should the unique "painter's eye" be made redundant?

How about going for a ride on your favorite scenic road—a beautiful wine route somewhere, with rolling hills and ever-changing vistas—only to find it has been replaced by a gap-reducing highway that is not only faster, but also boasts unobstructed views on all sides. Happy? Unobstructed views may stun you for a while, but imagination (and seduction) is dependent on the very distance and obstacle between you and your desired view—in other words, on the existence of gaps. Some of the most beautiful love poems were triggered by being away from the lover—should we do away with longing?

Gaps are not often invited into organizational life. When was the last time you saw a company's mission statement and values-of-our-organization poster say something like "We are committed to creating and maintaining the best gaps in customer service"? Most CEOs wish to have "one" organization, "united." Managers want employees to collaborate "closely," advancing "together" toward "well-defined" goals and reaching them "on time." Nothing in this ideal image of organization suggests any gaps. Indeed, if there's a gap somewhere, it's bad; it's a hazard to our unity. A gap in the organization means a problem, a bug, an error.

Precisely because gaps are often experienced as frightening, meaningless blanks in the work process or in communication, they are usually ignored—the elephant in the boardroom—in the hope that they will somehow disappear. If they continue to be an obstacle to unity, they are likely to be filled by more objects, stiff procedures, or just routine behavior.

Routine, by definition, is the most common "sealing" procedure. When we automatically, out of habit, use phrases we don't assign meaning to ("Let's get together sometime"), when a hollow gesture is performed as standard behavior only ("Smile!" for a camera), a tool does only what its manual says and nothing more is allowed ("Go to App Store"), and a person is faceless and labeled ("the cleaning lady"), we avoid gaps in perception. That's convenient. If we didn't do that, we'd have to start asking questions such as, Why can't I buy apps from another store?

What can this intelligent person who walks about the office all day cleaning teach me, the manager, that I cannot know by myself? Being afraid of the potential for havoc that gaps bring into our planned, orderly life, we tend either to ignore them (if they are only slight inconveniences) or suppress them (if they are traumatic, or too frightening). This is our way to cling to the past. Operating according to these patterns on a regular basis could prove a practical, comfortable way of living—but it comes with a price tag: It leaves no room for creativity. When we avoid gaps, we give up the possibility of choosing an interpretation for them, of putting them in context, of giving them a story. We also give up finding out their histories—and of giving them the future of our choice. To achieve that you would need to cultivate thinking through the gaps.

Embracing Gaps

What if, instead of denying gaps, one chooses to celebrate them? A jazz musician might happily say: "I had a great performance tonight, 'cause I've made all the *right* mistakes!" And right mistakes, mind you, are not the ones easily ignored or hidden. They are the ones that carry fresh discovery, innovation, and new potential. They are the ones that move you to make a positive change. Would you, in your organization, give up this resource of innovation? If not, hooray! You have just embraced your first gap.

Creativity in all forms of life, from arts to business to domestic situations, depends on our ability to recognize and explore gaps. Gaps are an opportunity to play with interpretations, with changing meanings. "Gap thinking" can contain a lot that "object thinking" rejects: the coexistence of contradictions, for one.

The reason gaps function so well as spaces for innovation is that, unlike objects, they are immaterial: They exist in our minds, memories, intuitions, and emotions— suggested, but not determined, by reality.

Any leader who yearns to master gap management should consider the example that the art world provides. Looking at works of art—in literature, poetry, painting, or even product design—we find that great works always create a unique gap between themselves and the conventions of the style of their time. Without this gap they are, well, standard. Even more impressive is the way every masterpiece opens a gap from the conventions set by earlier works of the same artist. Every symphony Beethoven wrote took a lot from his earlier works, but each of these great works contains an unpredictable element that sets it apart, makes it unique. This is why hundreds of symphonies written around the same time by lesser composers are forgotten today: They were composed according to the exact demands of the trendy late classical style, but they lacked what we may call the aesthetic gap—that necessary sufficient element of greatness. No one, even Beethoven himself, could have predicted the exact nature of those gaps before they materialized in his compositions. (In that sense, Beethoven himself was an exemplary ignorant maestro.)

Works of art that embody this aesthetic gap often meet with lack of understanding, even rejection, by the audience. When Tchaikovsky introduced his now beloved violin concerto, some critics considered it antimusic. When French Impressionism was in its infancy, it was excoriated by critics and influential citizens; many years passed before it became arguably the most popular painting style in modern history.

"And that is good: Art demands a period of confusion," the painter Yair Garbuz told me. "You see the work of a new painter and you say: What is this nonsense? Anyone can do it! Then in ten years it becomes a legitimate part of the discipline." During that period of time it has been assigned a meaning. If you want an equivalent from product design, remember the mockery that surrounded the first iPad—from its name to the claim that it was just "an oversized iPhone." In that case the creative gap was so big, it created a new category altogether. Many people simply could not understand what this new gadget meant.

So the difference between rejection and acceptance of the new, the innovative, is in the emergent meaning. We feel the need to assign meaning to what we recognize as a gap. If we fail, we regress to dismissal or denial. This is where leadership has its crucial role: to help search for meaning, and to support the process when the combined willpower of the stakeholders is not strong enough to do so. One may recall the very same role of Rancière's ignorant teacher.

So how does the leader fulfill this "midwife" role in the process? Assigning new meaning to gaps has to be an inclusive process, with many voices heard and as many stakeholders accepting ownership. However, in order to start the process of exploration, the leader has to put forward a leading concept to serve as scaffolding to the conversation. The use of metaphor is recommended due to its suggestive yet not defining power. For example, a conflict between two team members may be addressed using different metaphoric scaffolding: the team as "family" or as "combat unit" or "castaway" ship crew. Leadership needs to give sufficient orientation to enable progress, but not enough to restrict new or independent ideas. The leading metaphor may also change during the conversation, but it is necessary to start with a proposition, and the choice has great implications for its acceptance and the fertility of the discussion that follows. In a way, this first attempt at creating a platform for communication is an attempt at containing the gap, at creating a frame around it. It is a temporary structure that allows all the participants to look at it from all sides. Even before trying to create a meaning for the gap, the tools we are using to describe and contain it have great importance.

To illustrate, here is a story of a gap faced by an American industrial company that first opened its factory doors in 1836. Ensign-Bickford's first 150 years were focused primarily on developing safety fuses for explosives in order to protect miners. The technology was much later transformed into rocket science when the company created the explosives NASA used to launch rockets that send astronauts, weather satellites, and equipment for satellite radio into space. However, as the twenty-first century approached, mining companies ran into environmental and economic difficulties, and NASA cutbacks loomed. The company looked for ways to diversify.

In his travels for the company, one of EB's executives, Dave Malsbary, had met a scientist in the Midwest who had been doing experiments in his garage and had, quite by chance, come up with a new additive for dog food. In his informal tests—opening his garage to the neighborhood pets—his formula was apparently preferred by nine out of ten dogs over those of well-known brands.

Malsbary's proposal to the company's board, then,

was for EB to diversify by investing in pet food. One board member's reaction featured three words: "Are you nuts?" Another explained that EB was a company that had built its reputation on explosives and related products. How would producing dog food fit into such a business? In short, Malsbary faced a rather wide gap. It was a gap of expectation, history, perceived knowledge, and a clear skepticism of the idea that a sophisticated company should become ignorant and dive into unknown waters. How could he acknowledge that gap in a way that defined it, and how could he reframe the problem and solution in a way that would prove persuasive? He couldn't merely say, "It will be profitable." So would shoveling snow. He had to frame it in a way that showed both profitability and a fit within a bigger and an entirely sensible business plan.

Here's how he contained and reframed the gap. Yes, it would seem that pet food production doesn't make sense for a technology company. But over the years the company had proliferated by being creative and, in some ways, open-minded. Who would have thought, for example, that producing explosives would make it possible for radio listeners to tune into Beethoven symphonies or to rock concerts performed on distant continents—all through the magic of satellite radio? And what is the legacy of such technology? It is that EB had expanded its vision from addressing issues in a specific industry to enhancing the lives of people everywhere. In short, Malsbary argued that EB was already, in a sense, in the pet food business because it was in the lifestyle business, and pets are a big part of that. A stretch? Maybe. But the board bought it. And the resulting investment has yielded huge profits for Ensign-Bickford ever since. Not only that, but once it got into pet food, the door was opened to a warehouse of people food, also a profitable venture—and that would not have come about without Malsbary's proper gap treatment.

This openness to new meanings is the reason why gaps carry in them the possibility of indeterminacy, the freedom of choice, and therefore an open future. As a person working within an organization you might find the prospect a bit too open: What if various stakeholders in the organization end up in different "futures"? How shall we create unity? So here comes the real good news: Gaps well managed are not only likely to get you to unforeseen achievements in the future, they will also get you there united. United on many levels: as a business organization, as a family, even as a person divided between many interests and conflicting obligations.

How can gaps help create a stronger unity? The following story is very close to my heart for two obvious reasons: It is about my father, and it tells of my first musical memory that, in my adult mind, ties the two together to create an inspiring path toward unity.

My father was born in Jerusalem into a Syrian-Jewish family. His cultural world as an adult was diverse—rich with Judeo-Arabic religious heritage and literary tradition on one side, and on the other his love for European antiques and Japanese artifacts, and a wonderful collection of contemporary Israeli art he created with my mother—an outcome of a lifetime of active interest. Far from being trendy or showing off, his gentle personality was reflected in the diverse cultural mirrors that surrounded him. I often wonder how a harmonious personality like his could be composed, so to speak, of such diverse interests, capable of holding so many gaps.

To understand that I have to dive deep into my childhood experience, as I walked with my elder brother and my father to my grandfather's Sephardic synagogue in Jerusalem. It was then that I had the strange acoustical experience that constitutes my earliest musical memory.

Approaching the synagogue, I could clearly hear the melody of the prayer sung by the whole congregation—one strong, continuous stream of singing so beautiful that I rushed to open the door. Stepping in, however, I felt as if I were being pushed back by a massive wall of sound—noise, really, with only fragments of melody. I heard many individual voices loudly singing what I could gradually identify as independent variations of that same prayer melody. Each singer had different tuning and timing, and each was adding different embellishments, following the local tradition of his family's original hometown in the Diaspora, or just personal musical whim.

These people were not tone deaf, nor were they oblivious of the gaps in their singing: They were proudly presenting these gaps, the outcome of individualism within a strong tradition of a community that believed in inclusiveness. The prayer belonged to all, and everyone was invited to own it publicly.

I think my father's personality was shaped by his youthful experience of this community of many voices. He internalized its logic of inclusiveness in ways that allowed him to widen who he was, and to combine, naturally, respectfully, and with minimum internal friction, many diverse interests and loves. What enabled this rich combination was the fact that each of its components was characterized by gaps, and these gaps enabled his unity as a person, in the same way that gaps enabled the unity of his childhood community.

Now that I tell the story, other dear members of the family, on my mother's side, also come to mind. They were among the pioneers who established the first kibbutzim in Israel. The most nobly motivated (and naive) communist ideas led them to condemn any sign of individualism within their newly established society. Everyone thought, ate, dressed, and educated children exactly the same way.

Unity prevailed, great achievements were won—only to find out in a generation or two that this was not sustainable at all: Egalitarian ideology could not hide the gaps between individuals, and was a bad platform to deal with them successfully in the longer term. Where gaps are well treated, they create unity. Where gaps are denied, they may destroy unity.

In Sum, the Gap Leadership Challenge

The first step of the leader's challenge is to identify the most potent gaps, the ones that if well treated may bring about a significant positive change in the organization. This is not easy: The gaps with most potential are often the most intimidating ones, so they are probably covered with layers of tradition, routine, and "that's the way we've always done it here" attitude.

Once such a gap has been identified, it should be exposed and communicated to the organization. This is not a trivial or merely a technical endeavor, because denial of gaps and the fear of gaps are universal phenomena, far from being an attribute of leaders only. The communication should not be judgmental and should not shame or embarrass any of the stakeholders, because the process to come depends on their constructive participation.

Next, a frame should be presented and negotiated, one that can contain and hold the gap so that it can be studied and understood. Following that, the gap has to be assigned a meaning. Like any shared meaning, this has to be created together, in dialogue. If the gap is found to be meaningless by all stakeholders, it can be done away with: Just close it so it's not in the way (so we can concentrate on meaningful gaps). Most of the time, however, gaps have different meanings to different people, have different histories, and display different visions for the future. This is where the leadership role is the most difficult: having to lead a process in which the gap is not closed, and the stakeholders are willing to embrace ignorance, where no one claims ownership of "the truth." This delicate balancing act aims to create a new framework, a new perspective, in which the different meanings of the gap are woven together into a uniting narrative for the future, enabling the stakeholders to move on, change, and cooperate.

Sound complicated? But please consider the alternative, which is to dig trenches along the lines of conflicting interpretation, going nowhere. That grim prospect is a good enough reason to look at gaps and think of gaps differently. But there is one more skill that is required: keynote listening.

CHAPTER THREE

❧

Keynote Listening

Consider the standard practice of the keynote speaker: beginning each presentation with a joke or local anecdote. Perhaps it is about the cab ride from the airport or a reference to something that happened in town recently. Whatever it is, it's likely to be a crowd pleaser. Primed for a "serious" talk, the audience is relieved to know there is a real person up on the podium, who takes this seriously enough to provide a singular humorous introduction that makes a local reference. It is a win-win exchange between speaker and audience—sympathy in return for acknowledgment. This, in a nutshell, is the mechanism behind keynote speaking in general: It is a straightforward transaction. The obligatory joke ritual is performed in order to reassure everyone about their roles: active witty speaker, passive (and flattered, as witty) audience, ready to be entertained. It's safe and predictable, but it is also, to an extent, limiting.

If you want the people in your audience to become your partners, take an active part, assume responsibility for their own learning, and learn more of what you teach them—in short, if you want them to benefit from your ignorance as well as from your knowledge—you have to avoid falling into that pattern. You should transform the idea of a keynote speaker and become instead a keynote listener.

A keynote listener is no less focused than a keynote speaker, but his focal point is different. Instead of focusing on transmitting knowledge, he focuses on creating dialogue. The underlying belief is that the final learning of any interaction is different for each participant, and that the only way to enable each one to best process what she heard, to form her own ideas based on what she heard and share them with others, is through dialogue. The keynote listener holds the space in which the exchange is made, and the different learning "harvested" to the benefit of all. He, much like an ignorant teacher, verifies the process rather than the outcome. In fact, keynote listening is a key mode of action for an ignorant leader. Being "in the moment" is a key factor.

To illustrate and to show that keynote "listening" also involves other senses, let's go to the national conference hall in Budapest. The year is 2012, and I am about to give a lecture and conduct the Budapest Philharmonic. I am standing in the wings, adjusting my unruly hair, thinking about the music of Johann Strauss we are about to play and the 7,000 people in their seats, and going over what I had prepared as my introduction. Ah, and of that customary little joke, of course—something about my Hungarian nanny (a true story), some fifty years ago.

My cue is given, and I walk onstage, smiling, taking a bow. As I'm about to start speaking, and to introduce the memory of my Hungarian nanny, I notice something unusual: It is the face of the concertmaster, or rather his deeply astonished expression. This first violinist of the orchestra is a round, short man who has been very friendly and helpful during rehearsals—an excellent collaborator. But now, instead of what I expect to see—the normal professional sense of anticipation at the start of a show—his expression is very odd, a cross between serious purpose and crazy hilarity. He seems to have a face made of rubber, and he's beaming this half smile to me, to his fellow

musicians, and to the audience, which can see every nu-
ance as it is magnified a thousand times on the conference
hall's big screen. What exactly he's communicating I'm
not sure but I can't take my eyes off him, and neither can
anyone else. A worried voice in my head tells me to ignore
him and get going with my well-prepared routine—but
I'm simply too curious now. "What's with the face?" I say
half to him, half to the audience, genuinely lost as I am. It
is not in any script, but somehow I'm not panicking, because I can feel the power of being in the moment. I'm
trusting the audience to join in, drawn by the gap that was
just opened in my routine. The audience is indeed fully
engaged—we can feel it and hear it from the stage—and
this sets the tone for the entire performance.

Why did it work? Simply because the people in the
audience, the focal point of our efforts, are the most grateful when they are made to feel *alive*—when they can feel
they take part in something that is not "about something"
but is the thing itself. I would gladly define it with the
words: "being in awe of reality" (except that "reality TV"
has almost killed this word for us, along with the notion
of something being "awesome"). So we need keynote-
listening leadership to remind us of the now, of the possibility of life's constant unpredictability and of the power
of live dialogue.

One may wonder: How is dialogue possible between

one person onstage and 7,000 in the hall? My experience is that being "in dialogue" is like being ignorant, a mental disposition that one chooses, one that makes you look for nonverbal messages, even if hinted, sporadic, or short, much the way a lover would look for signs from his beloved or a parent from a baby—with extreme interest and heightened sensitivity.

But it doesn't require a room full of 7,000 people to apply these points, and discover the inherent values of extreme interest and heightened sensitivity. In our everyday lives we are reminded many times of the difficulties we make for ourselves when we don't listen, and yet it's a behavior that's hard to modify.

If you are, for example, a guest at a dinner party, you can hear for yourself just how extensive our nonlistening habits are. That is, we often don't use our ears to understand, or as tools to discover deeper meaning. When the host, for example, says the family has just returned from Paris and offers a highlight from the trip, at least three guests, though in the middle of the soup course, can't wait to express their own Paris experiences. Instead of probing the story of the host, making discoveries about his experience, they're busy rehearsing their own parts, only awaiting the host's final scene before launching into their own narratives.

Contrast this with, say, an ethic from days long ago

in economies much more modest when people around the dinner table were all ears. That is, the family could afford, perhaps, to send but one member to the matinee performance of a play or to the circus or the opera. And it was through that one family member that everyone else experienced the event—not only by listening to the narrative account, but by asking questions, encouraging discussion, and, in the end, feeling as if they had been there themselves.

As a leader, your choice for ignorance makes you focus on the learning processes of your people, supporting them in their autonomous discoveries. Your skill of keynote listening creates and holds a space for exchange, while your appetite for gaps sends you and them to find and create gaps, and use the energies stemming from those gaps for further exploration and exchange.

These elements are the ones that lead to a true connection to whoever your audience is: skeptical board members, shareholders, employees, or demanding bosses. Let's take a recent example from big industry to see how it works.

In 2013, a young man named Francesco Pagano invited me to lead a seminar at Mondelez International's European headquarters in Zurich (Mondelez is Kraft Foods outside North America). He explained that he

and his colleagues—all young middle managers—
wanted to change their company's culture before they
became too senior to care about anything other than
their seniority and hefty pay and, as a result, favored
new ideas only if they involved a minimum of risk.

When Francesco first joined Mondelez from a much
smaller company, he was impressed by its diversity. It
seemed like a great place to work except for one critical
aspect: He worried that the company wasn't nimble
enough to respond to a marketplace that was more com-
petitive and spontaneous than it had ever been. He won-
dered: Does everything at a big company have to be so
slow? Maybe he could help change the way the company
anticipated the ever-changing and challenging marketplace.

Senior management said (and created slogans for) all
the right things: "Act like owners"; "Discuss, decide, deliver"; "Tell it like it is"; "Be open and inclusive"; "Lead from
the head and from the heart." But as inspiring as these
words are, they were not consistently applied. Everyone in
middle management was aware of the gap between what
was said and what was done. Such a gap, of course, is
common in many companies: harboring lofty ideals that
do not drive everyday or even long-term decision making.
In Francesco's company, the gap he saw was generally

ignored; or worse, it created cynicism, the ultimate organizational poison.

But Francesco was a good listener, and he was not a cynic. He listened to the official messages and he chose to believe them. So he started echoing the messages he believed in, in good faith, back to his managers, where they came from. This alone, he discovered, had some power.

Then Francesco listened to the internal frustration and noticed where it was coming from. It wasn't coming from the executive offices. People who sat in those chairs felt fine. It came from his group of middle managers who could hear the discord between the way things were and what could be. That was a positive force. They were not moaning or complaining—they simply wanted their company to act on its ideals. But to be effective, Francesco knew they would have to come together. He exposed the gap, making it visible so that his management and colleagues could take action.

The rest was easy. Senior management agreed to bring young, innovative managers from all over the world to a conference they initiated and curated themselves— not another top-down HR dutiful event, but an effort owned by its participants.

The event's mission was to empower middle managers—and in turn, those around them—to discard the "can't do" attitudes that threaten every bureaucracy. Francesco, then, found a way to make routine words actually mean something.

That conference's impact has been felt everywhere in Mondelez and certainly in Francesco's department. "We now give regular presentations on what it means to be an innovative company, to be more fluid, to respond to the marketplace, not through years of testing and being sure but by taking more risk and being quicker on our feet."

Francesco is now re-creating this innovative mindset globally. And here's the biggest surprise: One day, Francesco got a call from his innovation counterpart at one of the most innovative companies on earth: Google. Could Google people come to visit and learn from him?

So it was Francesco's determination and his ability to give voice to the gap and create energy out of the evolving dialogue (for which he created a platform)—all these made the difference. Francesco did not have a specific innovation or product he wanted to push, so he was ignorant about where it would all lead. He focused on holding the space open instead of on the outcome. In musical terms I would claim that Francesco made sure that all the sections of the orchestra were audible to the degree that the discords had to be dealt with, and he listened in a way that made others listen while those discords were being transformed into a web of connected melodies. In this respect his work echoes that of a conductor.

To a leader, one of the more rewarding aspects of keynote listening is that it creates great speakers and more listeners. The fact is that when you are being listened to by a keynote listener, the way you speak is changed. You no longer try to fit your words and ideas into some existing categories you deem to identify at your listener's end, but you are given the freedom to venture into uncharted territories, knowing you have the safety net of listening. This is a safe space in which mistakes are welcomed, sorted out, and used as learning. On an even more basic level, your listener acknowledges you as a legitimate, equal contributor. That alone goes a very long way, as this next story will show.

Moshe Talgam, my father, was a senior judge at the Tel Aviv district courthouse. Many rough outlaws were brought before him for sentence. Some of those convicted ended up in prison for many years for crimes such as murder, rape, or armed robbery.

One particularly tough nut the justice system had to cope with was the infamous Alperon family case. The Alperons formed a ruthless crime organization, known for its brutality: The name itself was sufficient threat to produce extortion money, and if that didn't work, they were known for their use of violence—from knives to explosives. Once brought to trial, their behavior in the court of law made it impossible to conduct a trial. They refused to keep silent—they constantly made loud noise, singing and shouting, so it became impossible to examine witnesses. They could not be tried in their absence, however, because of the severity of the accusations. There was simply no way to make them cooperate, and more than one judge had to resign from their case, unable to complete the proceedings.

The case finally landed with my father. He did not threaten the Alperons with further sanctions. He did not even order them to listen: He just listened to them. He gave them all the time they needed to express themselves. He listened to their words, but even more he listened to their inner motivations, to their self-perception as human beings in conflict. He listened empathically, though not sympathetically. He didn't let his legal knowledge of what was acceptable as evidence in court block him from listening to the story the way they wanted to tell it. He understood that sometimes a lot more has to be said, and listened to, in order for justice not only to be done but also to be understood as justice by the very people who are about to be punished. To everyone's amazement, the court proceedings went smoothly, with no provocations or clashes. The judge respects us, so we return this respect—that was their natural reaction. They appreciated being given the chance to be judged and sentenced out of respect for their humanity, rather than being put down as the scum of the earth. It was not about the severity of their final sentence, but about their being invited to take part in the process.

Keynote listening was not a tactical trick on my father's side—that wouldn't have worked, as they were experienced and sophisticated. As all leadership is manifested in the leader's being, my father was simply listening to them as he always did—that was part of his being. As his listening changed attitudes and behaviors of other people, I think he was a true keynote listener.

On a truly historic scale, an epic leader can use large-scale keynote listening against the background of a tragic gap to move his nation in a peaceful path toward a better future. The story of apartheid in South Africa is well known, as is the story of Nelson Mandela's fight against it.

What sets Mandela apart from many heroic freedom fighters is his choice when the fighting was over. "As I walked out the door toward the gate that would lead to my freedom, I knew if I didn't leave my bitterness and hatred behind, I'd still be in prison," he famously said.

As the new leader of the postapartheid nation, he could, by every right, push for justice: punish the oppressors and compensate the oppressed. By that means he would, symbolically and in practice, close the gap of injustice—level the gains and losses.

Mandela chose differently. Leveling human political rights came with the end of apartheid, but the heavy burden of the long history of apartheid had to be confronted— this gap could not be ignored or forgotten. Mandela understood that trying to close this mental gap with revenge-driven punishment and compensation was bound to fail. These "filling materials" wouldn't do, because there was not enough justice to go around: How much compensation was sufficient for ruining the lives of millions for so long? He understood the need to hold the gap, leave it open, explore it by listening to the stories from both sides. To do that, the Truth and Reconciliation Commission— which could grant amnesty to people who came before it and confessed their politically motivated crimes—came into being. (In extreme cases it could also deny amnesty.) The commission gave the victims of such crimes a voice to tell their stories. People from all sides were now listening. No one, in my opinion, Mandela included, could have predicted the outcome of these proceedings, and yet it is generally accepted today that this commission was an essential component in the success of the transition to the new political era in South Africa. Mandela's leadership succeeded in creating a noble and lasting legacy for the whole world by holding a tragic and violent gap, being a keynote listener promoting listening under the most difficult circumstances, and acting out of human-trusting ignorance.

Part
THREE

Six Musical Variations on the Themes of Leadership

Consider, if you would, the implications of two disparate definitions of the job of conductor:

From Elias Canetti, philosopher: "His eyes hold the whole orchestra. Every player feels that the conductor sees him personally and, still more, hears him. . . . He is inside the mind of every player. He knows not only what each should be doing but what he is doing. He is the living embodiment of law, both positive and negative. His hands decree and prohibit. . . . And since, during the performance, nothing is supposed to exist except this work, for so long is the conductor the ruler of the world."

From André Previn, conductor: "What is the conductor for? Well, I think first of all for the over-simplified reason of just being the traffic cop; you know—making sure that everyone is playing at the same speed and at the same volume."

A job description containing both the omnipotent "ruler of the world" and the mundane duty of "traffic cop" seems self-contradictory, yet both portrayals hold truth about an inherent gap within the conductor's leadership role.

On one hand, compliance with the rules concerning every technical aspect of the playing has to be ensured and accounted for: the tuning of each instrument, the intonation of different instruments, coordinated playing, the exact timing and character of the beginnings, evolution, and endings of sounds—millions of details in an average symphonic piece that together, if well managed, result in quality playing. This is not unlike making sure traffic flows safely, or even, on a larger scale, of managing the elaborate logistics of a supply chain, getting thousands of components to the assembly line in perfect timing to sustain the flow of manufacturing.

On the other hand, above making sure rules are

kept, conducting contains an element of creation, of making sense of a higher order and communicating that sense. The many details must create a sum not only greater than its components (every machine assembled will fulfill that requirement)—but of a totality of a different quality: that of a living entity rather than that of a machine. Since assembling a machine is different from creating an organism, the living body of an orchestra should follow the same principles of interdependence and growth—both cultivated but not directly controlled by management.

The handling of a multitude of simultaneous events could prove tricky for any manager or conductor. If she tries to manage all the numerous details of the performance, cue all the dozens of different parts and instruments, and give proper feedback in real time, she will soon find herself chasing after the music rather than managing it—like Charlie Chaplin on the speedy assembly line in his classic film *Modern Times*. On the other hand, if her vision of grand design disconnects entirely from the earthly world of proper production, again, she will soon lose control—this time more like *The Sorcerer's Apprentice* in *Fantasia*, where the dreaming wannabe sorcerer, poor Mickey, is awakened by the flood created by his own charmed "employees," threatening to drown him.

Leadership, including both management and vision,

is needed in order to not be drowned by details or get lost seeking Utopia.

So our goal should be to understand both the message of leadership and its delivery. These are not disconnected. Many times the strongest message is *in* the delivery, not apart from it. If content and form are not aligned, a discrepancy is created—a gap. Like any gap, this may prove useful—if it is understood and regarded by the leader as a call to find better ways to communicate his intentions. But it is not useful if it becomes a reason for the followers to doubt the leader's authenticity.

Delivery, the communication of a message, has a lot to do with what we identify as "personal style." Style is always something more than its components and it is immediately recognizable, just as the sound of your favorite hard-rock band is the first element you recognize, even if you only hear it for a second or two, even before you recognize the song. This is why some orchestral players claim to know whether someone is a good conductor just by watching that person walking from the stage door to the conductor's podium. That assertion might be a bit too hasty, but they are quick to recognize style. When style works, it's called personality. When it works wonderfully, it's called charisma. Leonard Bernstein had charisma. So did Lee Iacocca, former CEO of Chrysler; the late Steve Jobs; and

Jack Welch, former CEO of General Electric. Bill Gates? Not so much, but he makes up for it in other ways.

Style has many manifestations, from the countless aspects of body language, of which posture, facial expression, and hand gestures are the most obvious, to verbal communication, including the music of one's speech— tone, pace, pauses—as much as one's actual choice of words. Moreover, style is manifested through ways of interaction with the physical and social environment.

As for the all-important authenticity of style, certain manifestations of style can be imitated, no doubt. You can speak the way someone in authority speaks, or walk the way someone sexy does—it's mostly good for making people laugh. People laugh more when the imitation is perfect, precisely because of the discrepancy between what is implied and what they know the imitator actually to be. Sometimes imitations go deeper: The imitator is internalizing and using the same gestalts of speech, structures of conversation—often not even being aware of it—as his model. In extreme cases people will indeed identify the imitator as "the real thing."

I was a student in a conducting class in Fontainebleau, near Paris, where our revered teacher, Leonard Bernstein, and all of his students were watching one of our colleagues conducting an orchestra. I remember watching with growing envy. This student conductor was making exactly the same gestures as Bernstein—and I don't mean just the hand technique—everything was there, perfectly executed: the jumping, the groans, the faces, the heavy breathing. I thought I saw an incarnation of the maestro. While immersed in envy and self-pity (I wanted so much to be able to do that!), I heard Bernstein, right in front of me, turn around and say, not loudly but deliberately: "This guy thinks he is like me—but I am not an imitator."

You could easily be impressed, say, by the practices of certain business leaders, and try to follow their example, measure by measure. Jack Welch, whose tenure at General Electric and whose books on leadership have made him an icon, is known as an executive who connects on a person-to-person basis in part because he remembers the name of everyone he meets. This astounds and impresses everyone, and makes them feel important. Wouldn't you want to do that? But Welch's gift is a rare one, not easily copied. The point is not to wish you were like someone else (Woody Allen said, "My only regret in life is that I'm not someone else") but to play your singular strength as a leader. That's what this section of the book is about—determining where you will find yourself on a wide spectrum of leadership styles, understanding how your own unique mix of strengths can serve you best in an organizational context. But there is one element that can't be missing from your leadership solution—it's the authentic you.

Leadership style has to be embedded in the "being" of the leader. It has to be perceived as authentic. If, in true admiration, you try to be General Patton or Lyndon Johnson you are bound to fail—unless you are using those great figures as scaffoldings for personal growth and are letting go of them once you have exhausted their learning potential. Consider, perhaps, the journeys of entertainers Rich Little and Sammy Davis, Jr. Both could impersonate dozens of famous people. But, in the long run, Little is lost among the stars—no authentic personality of his own. Sammy Davis, Jr., found, after many years, his own voice, his own way of communication—he no longer had to be someone else.

Perceived authenticity in a leader is critical if she wants her message genuinely to reach and touch the receiver. Without it, the message will be met and distorted by distrust or cynicism, to the point of becoming counterproductive.

The question of authenticity as applied to the leadership styles of orchestra conductors is sharpened by the fact that orchestras differ from most other organizations in that their work is divided into rehearsal and performance.

It is true that leadership could, and does, change its manifestations when exposed to the gaze of the general public. The extent of that change is very individual and in itself dependent on style. Authentic leadership, however, is tested by the way this change is perceived by the players, who experience both ends: If they can detect an inner cause for it—as opposed to the conductor's putting on a show for the clients—then leadership is unharmed. Rehearsal is often a cause for envy for managers in fields other than performing arts.

"We never get time to rehearse—we perform all the time!" is a statement I often hear from many in various industries. They wish they had the time to prepare better, individually and as a team, before they have to perform complicated tasks, some of them for the first time in the presence of demanding clients or critical bosses. I empathize with this wish, precisely because our rehearsals are always demanding tests for conductors, where the conductor is judged by musicians on many levels, and for the orchestral players, who are supposed to master their difficult parts before they come to the rehearsal. The conductor's disadvantage is that he cannot rehearse for his rehearsals: They only happen in real time. Of course a conductor can and should prepare, by simulating certain aspects, as one would run scenarios in his head for a conversation he is about to have. So it would make sense to claim that in leading an orchestra, as in leading a business, every activity is a performance as much as it is, or should be, a rehearsal for the next activity.

An Observatory of Conducting Stars

What follows are the results of observing six great conductors at work, and relating their methods to matters far beyond the concert hall. These are my observations, and so they are far from being untouched by my own beliefs or even taste, but they do incorporate the accumulated experience of watching these conductors' video clips and discussing them with tens of thousands of people during the last twenty years or so.

I chose these conductors for being among the brightest stars of the visually documented era of conducting. Each of them has become an icon of excellence in music making. Even more important for the purpose of this book, each of them fits as an archetype of a certain leadership style. In this context, each projects a clear and distinct worldview, a coherent set of beliefs, which in turn generates a working principle by which they operate, exercise influence, and measure success for themselves.

These conductors' leadership styles were not shaped in a void: They are the products of the cultural forces of their particular times and geographies—affected by nationality, school, language, economics, and politics—but, simultaneously, they also shaped the culture of their organizations, and often their influence has gone much further than that, to become a mirror and catalyst in society at large.

One huge void in the following set of conductors is the lack of women. This, unfortunately, represents the state of affairs in the sphere of star conductors throughout the profession's history. Why this was and still is largely the case (despite some remarkably talented exceptions) is certainly not irrelevant to understanding leadership, but gender issues are, alas, beyond the scope of this book. Patterns of behavior that are stereotypically regarded as masculine or feminine are, however, very much present in our discussion.

CHAPTER FOUR

Command and Control: Riccardo Muti

Riccardo Muti, an extremely elegant man, walks into the pit of the opera house as if under a glass bell, his expression serious and concentrated. Utterly unaffected by the cheering and clapping of the audience, seemingly obeying only his inner pulse, he takes his place on the podium. His perfect Latin posture emphasizes, almost justifies, his central position, between orchestra, stage, and audience.

Mozart's opera *Don Giovanni* is announced by heavy

blocks of sound produced by the full forces of the orchestra, sounds that summon the spirit of a murdered knight, the Commendatore. These chords are born in and fade out into silence. They need great energy to come into being. Riccardo Muti is not looking for that energy anywhere around him—not in the expectations of his players or in the tense silence of the audience. Rather, it seems to come out of Muti's completely autonomous being, as if he were a precharged battery, discharging into the orchestra.

Muti commands the first chords with sharp and strong arm movements. No detail is left unaccounted for in his gestures, and every change in the music is projected to the orchestra well before it is actually due. Muti controls and supervises every move, by everyone. He cuts off the sound so forcefully that—even after the players have long stopped playing—his hands keep trembling with great effort, as if in a struggle.

As observers we ask ourselves what underlies this struggle, and what can we learn about Muti as a leader from that intense moment. Is Muti struggling with a *technical* difficulty, as the sound itself refuses to die out? Is he engaged with the *meaning* behind that sound, experiencing the drama of fighting the dead Commendatore? Or is he actually establishing his own control over the orchestra? Well, imagine yourself having a new boss like Muti. In his first week in the office, he or she is already so heavily invested in struggle that you have to ask yourself: Is this new boss interested in contributing to *how* we do things? Will the new boss help us rethink *why* we do them? Or is this boss interested largely in securing a powerful position in the game of company politics?

The answer presents itself as Muti's performance of *Don Giovanni* continues. Two and a half hours or so into the opera, while conducting the final scene in which everybody celebrates having finally got rid of the rebel-murderer-womanizer Giovanni, Muti still wears the same unchanging expression on his face and makes the same sharp, commanding hand gestures that have nothing to do with the dramatic narrative. His gestures seem to be more a sign of his leadership style than a response to a technical need or a visualization of the character of the music. They are mostly about what Muti conceives as the core of his duties as conductor: He has to be in *control*.

His control is top-down, but it originates from even higher above: By his own testimony, Muti sees himself under the control of the musical "lawmaker"—and deviating from the law is a crime. He feels constantly judged by some unforgiving superego—perhaps the spirit of Mozart (or any other great composer whose music he performs)—holding Muti fully accountable for delivering a faithful execution of his score. It's not unlike a company CEO, being under the constant scrutiny of the board of directors and publicly demonstrating the desire to please that board. Muti rises to the challenge, armed with a clear leadership formula (which he claims to be in the tradition of Toscanini), meaning that the conductor should always have sole authority as the senior representative of the composer—even in an opera production, which has so many sides that are not directly musical: stage design, lighting, costumes. His proposal is clear-cut: He will take full responsibility, and in return he demands full control. Not just self-control, but control of every detail in the process of executing the one and only correct interpretation—his.

As an instrument of control, Muti is formidable. He's like a human panopticon or a supervisor's mirror glass office, from which he could be watching you at all times. His body firm on his legs, which seem independent of the strong movements of the arms, enables his erect head to watch steadily over the players without losing the slightest detail. His commanding gestures often have a degree of repetition about them, as if not leaving any chance of misunderstanding on the part of the players.

Imagine you're having a short and clear conversation with your boss concerning a very specific detail of your work. As you leave the room you get a text reminder from her to your phone, then an e-mail, a phone call from her secretary, and a fax is waiting on your table . . . not very trusting, is it? Muti's directions always come well ahead of time, as he is busy controlling the next event, rather than sharing with his players the events in the music as they happen. So much effort goes into securing the delivery of his instructions that one wonders: What could happen if, for a little while, there were no instructions? In other words—if Muti, as the CEO of a company, took three days off, would his company collapse? Doesn't he have enough trust in his players' abilities to conduct themselves for even the shortest while? It seems that whatever Muti thinks about his employees' abilities, his fear of losing control, inevitably followed by mistakes, still takes over. Mistakes cannot be tolerated, as they represent a betrayal of his core responsibility to the lawmaker, the composer.

Since Muti does not trust his players to self-organize, it follows that he must make his messages to them overwhelmingly clear. This is why he keeps beating time, always visible to all. This is like leading a marching band or beating the bass drum: It forces everyone to play together. This comes, however, at the cost of sacrificing more subtle aspects of the playing. Imagine a melody as a beautiful line drawn by a master painter—the line has character and life, far from being a line created by connecting dots to produce a preconceived shape in a drawing book. Musicians also must strive to give the notes a continuous life, full of intensity and direction. Muti is so concerned with getting to the "milestones" that he might almost forget to look beyond the mileage gauge and actually enjoy the ride.

Is conducting a happy experience for Muti? In reply to an interview question, complimenting him for "looking so majestic, like a king on his throne," Muti is almost appalled: "You call this podium a throne? I call it an island of solitude."

This joyless reply should not surprise us, since we can appreciate the Sisyphean nature of trying to eliminate gaps. The idea of command and control has no tolerance for gaps, and demands constant effort to suppress them. In its fundamental form, so well exemplified by Muti, the imminent failure to do so is crushed or denied. Leaders may ignore the gap between themselves and the lawmakers, because acknowledging this gap means that their interpretation might not be superior to their followers', hence a threat to their authority. They strive to eliminate the gap of control by providing an endless series of directions, micromanaging every aspect of the work, so as not to leave employees to their own direction even for the shortest while. In this the leader minimizes his followers' space, and, paradoxically, his own space too. The business of controlling and commanding never pauses, and leaders simply cannot free themselves from constantly issuing instructions.

Most of us will probably identify with Muti's dislike

of mistakes, as they are the gap between what we meant to get and what came out, a result of our imperfect control. But what if the mistake actually brought about something *better* than we planned? The crucial gap contains the possibility of looking at mistakes as potential gains. Penicillin would not have been recognized if Alexander Fleming, like researchers before him, had thrown away the contaminated petri dish. When Muti closes the door on a gap, which might offer a "safe space" in which, within the right parameters, mistakes are *welcomed* as a way of creativity and search for self-expression, he puts a limit on his orchestra's best possible performance. A generic musician's joke captures Muti in a nutshell: "How was your concert with Muti?" the concertmaster of one orchestra was asked by a friend. "It was fine," he said. "It could have been better, but he wouldn't let us."

No doubt you can recognize the chilling effect on everyday business life when the mantra becomes "This is what the boss wants, period." Or, even worse, "This is what the boss doesn't want—so never do it." In the newspaper business, "Dog bites man" isn't news. "Man bites dog," on the other hand, is the definition of news. But what happens when publisher bites editor?

By 1970, the *Akron Beacon Journal* had long been considered one of the country's leading regional newspapers. It was the first paper run by the legendary journalism figure John S. Knight (of Knight-Ridder fame). He was an old-fashioned newsman who wore a fedora, a double-breasted suit, and a serious expression to the corner office. He was about to retire then but still had great influence.

One day, the paper published a photograph of a dog on page one. Knight later told the paper's editor that he *didn't like* the photograph. Quickly, the editor called a meeting of top-level newsroom management and declared that never again would a picture of a dog go on page one. It wouldn't matter if there were a photograph of the pope biting his schnauzer. There was now a prohibition.

This was not, of course, the great John S. Knight's intention at all. On the other hand, he bears some responsibility for what happened. He put a chill in the air. Editors considered his view to be the one from the mountaintop. He had proclaimed from on high, they felt, what the gods of journalism intended—"The Pursuit of Truth, Justice, the American Way, and Never Putting a Dog on Page One." John S. Knight, in that way, was a Riccardo Muti. He had a great number of strengths, but the ability to welcome gaps in a healthy fashion wasn't among them. Or to put it another way: What's the point of having an organization of educated and talented people if they are not empowered to form independent opinions and put them in play? So, then, the embracing of gaps and, moreover, the creation of gaps is a key to liberating thought and bringing about positive changes.

When Muti creates gaps, he touches greatness. Ironically, these gaps are sometimes created thanks to his authoritative and disciplinary gap-hating attitude. This is an account of his first rehearsal with the Israel Philharmonic, which I attended.

The IPO is a wonderful orchestra, with working habits that draw on Mediterranean and Middle Eastern cultures and, perhaps, the Indian origin of its musical director, Zubin Mehta, almost as much as they draw from its great European tradition. One symptom of this mixture is a certain lack of formal discipline and disregard for hierarchy. Mehta, a native of Bombay, jokingly said: "In this orchestra I'm the only Indian. All the others are chiefs!" In addition to these lively characteristics of the ensemble, the local audience refuses to take concert hall etiquette very seriously. For example: Coughing during concerts seems to be a global problem, but nowhere like here. The famous pianist Arthur Rubinstein once said: "Everywhere in the world when people have the flu they go to a doctor—in Tel Aviv they come to my concerts."

I went to watch Muti's first encounter with the orchestra, wondering how the clash between the two work cultures might end. I have to say it was a knockout for

Muti. His reputation preceded him; the hundred or so angelic faces of musicians looking at him as he entered the stage were the first sign of his victory. Not a single multitasking musician showed up: no texting on a smartphone or gossiping—in itself a highly remarkable phenomenon for an orchestra composed almost entirely of people who, it might be surmised, consider following rules an option.

Muti raised his baton for the first upbeat—that preparatory cue for the orchestra—and just then, in that moment of intense silence, one of the players (who apparently could not see the rather short conductor very well) moved his chair, and this minor furniture rearrangement resulted in a loud scratching noise. Muti's hands froze halfway. He looked at his score, then he looked at the players, and then he said in a low yet very deliberate voice: "Gentlemen, I don't have a scratch of a chair in my score!" That was it—from then on you could hear a dead fly in the auditorium. For the whole length of the rehearsal there was such complete silence, the music making aside, that for the first time in years the Israel Philharmonic could actually *hear itself playing.* In the course of ten minutes the orchestra had reached a level better than it had attained in years. Muti had succeeded in creating for the Israel Philharmonic the one element they lacked in order to play like a great orchestra—*silence.*

Thus Muti opened a potent gap between the mundane, routine, unconscious behavior of the orchestra to something new, which enabled excellence and, ultimately, joy for everyone, the orchestra and its coughing audience alike.

It may be true that from Muti's point of view he closed the gap between his expectation for discipline and the orchestra's "normal" behavior. Still, from the orchestra's point of view he created new reality and consequently a gap in perception. We may presume that if Muti were to become the permanent conductor of the orchestra, this gap would cease to exist, along with his magical influence on the playing. That moment of first encounter embodied the perfect case of the right leader for the needs of the followers. As these needs keep changing they should trigger a change in what leadership supplies, and keynote listening is needed to enable this looping back and learning on the part of the leader.

When I give seminars to business leaders and, after watching videos of Muti, I ask, "How many of you would like to have him as your boss?" an average of only 1 or 2 percent of the audience will raise their hands. The same goes for people in all other professions; Muti is hardly a smashing success in that context, ever. The curious thing is that for the same audience, when asked "Will he deliver? Get the job done?" about 90 percent are convinced he will. The root of this seeming lack of coherence is not that most people resent being pushed to results. The problem, many feel, is that discipline and strictness can quickly deteriorate into bullying. Is Muti a bully?

I don't think he is. I should know, because I have studied and worked with a bullying conductor (more on that in the next chapter). As for Muti, my glimpses of his off-podium communication are what makes me like him: I see a self-conscious, self-doubting, and humorous man, a man full of gaps. And, as a conductor of great musicality and charisma, he is admired for his results. Still, on the podium, Muti is stuck in his mode of leadership that people, given the choice, would not like to adopt. Often people say something like: "Sure, it's efficient—but only good for the military!" Obviously they refer to the army as an epitome of an organization built on stiff hierarchy and discipline, characterized by no tolerance for disobedience. But is "the army" really a fitting slot for Muti's style? My own military service, some thirty-five years ago, taught me otherwise.

In Israel, a country then as now in constant conflict with its neighbors, the army experience is part of every citizen's life. The obligatory military service is the great social melting pot where you meet people from very different life circumstances. Army service is where many Israelis, including most of the country's political leaders, had their first taste of leadership, and also where the highly creative high-tech companies that gave the country its "start-up nation" nickname are born. I also had my first training in leadership in officers school, and as a lieutenant in a combat unit during times of relative quiet along the borders, I enjoyed long stretches of lazy routine, which I spent reading—*Catch-22* was our bible at the time— interrupted only by a stream of commands from my distant battalion's headquarters, most of which I found to be unnecessary or even counterproductive. Luckily, unlike Joseph Heller's crazily irrational world, the Israeli army (or at least its field units) offered an environment in which you called your commanding officers by their first names, almost never mentioning a person's rank, and rarely took commands at face value. There was always room for negotiation—and not only by the likes of me, a junior officer. My soldiers, too, made their opinions about everything well known to me, and if they felt I was ignoring their opinions, they would respond by ignoring my commands. I realize this account of army life might sound surprising and even extreme, but it is accurate, as far as my experience goes. There were limits to "negotiations," and as an officer you were expected to decide, even make unpopular decisions, or you would lose the respect of your people. But you had to listen and act from there—not just listen for the protocol—and gain their attention and obedience.

How would a Muti type fit in this environment? Generally speaking, the Muti types I encountered enjoyed very little esteem from subordinates, with the exception of those few commanders who had legendary reputations as leaders in combat, and then, on condition that their Muti style was restricted to operational issues. Friction and disobedience emerged whenever "discipline" was applied to other issues, such as dress code and haircuts.

My youthful experience in active service was not irrelevant for the challenge presented when two generals of the Israeli army's northern command came to see me one evening in early 2013, asking for my advice. The gap they described was between opposing perceptions of the relations between the generals of the command's headquarters on one hand and the commanding officers of the fighting divisions on the other.

As I was given to understand, the fighters wanted to be, in effect, like jazz soloists with only a minimum of written instruction and most of the music improvised. The generals at headquarters wanted something more like a big band, or even a marching band, in which very little is left to improvisation and almost everything is prearranged to make the maximum effect by coordinated use of resources. It was clearly an issue of leadership, and my visitors knew that exercising sanctions against unruly commanders would not solve it. They asked me to come up with something that would lend a new perspective to the problem and allow for new thoughts and behaviors from all stakeholders. They didn't know what this approach could be, and I admired them for their self-imposed ignorance concerning it. As they wanted something really new, they realized they should not suggest, even predict, a line of action. They entrusted me with the challenge, and a four-hour session was scheduled a week later, all parties invited.

I flew from Tel Aviv to a small airfield near the Golan Heights, where the Israel Defense Forces' northern command generals were assembled. One of them met me outside. He preferred not to stay for the session because, he said, he always fell asleep during academic lectures, embarrassing himself and frustrating the lecturer. I assured him I was not an academic or a lecturer, and that I wasn't even going to teach him anything—I would just show him something. A bit perplexed, he agreed to stay.

That was my idea: I would put in front of them a challenging leadership model, but one inseparable from an equally challenging teamwork model. They would have to consider a leadership perspective completely immersed in the practice of cooperation on the highest level.

I invite you now to imagine a quite surreal scene. Only a few miles away from a raging battle between the rebel forces and the Syrian army in that terrible civil war, a tight circle of senior Israeli army men is sitting around four young musicians, a string quartet, playing pieces by Brahms and Mozart. I had arranged for these four excellent players to be surprise guests.

Why? What makes a classical string quartet a suitable thought-provoking model for a team of army commanders? The key elements are that, through the operation, every member of the team is both a soloist and a leader, and "success" depends on total cooperation.

The functions of each of the four parts may change momentarily. At any given moment, a player could be playing the solo tune or a secondary melody or an accompaniment figure or just pause. You may assume that playing the "solo" melody automatically gives you license to follow your own pulse only. Not so, as rhythm is actually dictated by the accompanying parts (think of a solo guitar "riding" on the pulsating drum kit of a rock band, if you will). Intonation (playing in tune) and color (quality of sound) are two other elements that may be suggested simultaneously by different players. As in a giant kaleidoscope, constantly changing, the team members must quickly identify their position and role, not just in terms of their written part but taking into account everyone else's playing in real time, and responding to deviations from preconceived agreements. The written score suggests these changing responsibilities, but the way of execution has to be decided upon by the players, forging a joint interpretation out of their individual views.

These insights came up in the conversation between the two ensembles—musicians and commanders. The musical cooperation was being described and analyzed by the two groups, comparing their findings using two different vocabularies. Luckily, they did not think their disciplines were "just the same"; that would mean there was nothing new to learn. Instead, the gaps between "military speak" and "musical speak" were studied. For example, the give-and-take relations between melody and accompaniment were compared to the relations between the attacking force and its logistical support, finding similarities and differences and gaining new perspectives. What resulted was described by the reluctant "sleepy" general: "It was a revelation. I was able to see myself through them, as an unexpected reflection in a hall of mirrors."

As a final question to the members of the quartet, I asked them if they would welcome a conductor to lead them—an offer they all declined very emotionally: "It would get between us and the music, we don't need anyone to tell us what to do!" And what if he didn't tell you what to do, but made observations and suggestions? This they all welcomed, "on condition he's a really good musician." And if the ensemble was larger, like an orchestra?

Then "we definitely need a conductor to hold the discussion, and decide." This suggested a kind of leadership that the army men seemed happy to consider for themselves, and very far from the Muti-military stereotype.

I suspect that sometimes Muti himself would prefer not to be a Muti type, in light of what was probably the worst moment in his career. By 2005, Muti had already been the music director of Italy's best-known opera house, La Scala of Milan, for nineteen years. He became involved in a power play over certain decisions (heavily politicized, as is always the case in Italy). At one point Muti declared he would not conduct until his demands were fulfilled, hoping for the orchestra's support for his cause. Instead, the orchestra and staff overwhelmingly approved a motion of "no confidence in the music director." Shocked and hurt by this betrayal by his own troops, Muti resigned.

Why didn't the musicians back him? Because although the performances were good, they felt he was using them like instruments, not partners in interpretation. They didn't have to study the music, just follow instructions. Under these conditions, even the most ardent love and devotion to music will fade in the long run, causing the musicians and the opera house great damage.

Or as another commentator, Norman Lebrecht, one of today's greatest experts on conducting, wrote: "The opera world has got used to Muti's limited vocabulary, an emotive lexicon lacking in compromise. There is only one way to work with Muti: his way."

Muti is still one of the most sought-after conductors in the world. Has he any new thoughts about conducting, particularly after feeling betrayed by his musicians?

The following is a monologue by Riccardo Muti delivered while rehearsing with the London Philharmonic Orchestra, presenting what sounds like a complete renunciation of not only his own dictatorial behavior but of the whole conducting profession.

While the orchestra is playing a piece by Dvořák, Muti stops the music. He says, "*È molto importante*, this passage, from C major to A-flat major: You, as musicians, you have to find the color inside you . . ." (He sings the passage they are rehearsing, then makes a gesture of change) ". . . I can't do anything . . . I can try to do a beautiful face—that is impossible for me" (laughter from orchestra) "and I'm not doing nothing, it's *you* who are doing, trying very hard—to play" (sings, looking at the players) "—trumpets, and violins . . . so I will try to do *nothing* . . . and you just go from *Do maggiore* to *La bemolle maggiore* . . ." (some clapping from players).

How wonderful, and tragic. Wonderful because Muti acknowledges the individual, autonomous search by every one of his players for the right interpretation—far beyond simple execution. He legitimizes their efforts, and empowers them—even at the expense of his control. Why tragic? Because Muti cannot forgo the binary thinking: one or zero. Either I tell you everything (as he usually does) or else I am a redundant and pathetic figure, making funny faces for the camera. The third option—that of leading by empowering others to lead, so beautifully brought to life by Muti in his monologue above—he still cannot recognize as "conducting." The result is that he must renounce his own identity as conductor to allow the music to be saved by his musicians.

Is there hope for a Muti type to change? It is common wisdom that the greatest obstacle to changing yourself is success, while failure can be a great motivator to look for a new way. Failure by itself may push Muti types to extremes: Either they become Super-Mutis or commit a symbolic suicide. If, however, Muti types can be helped to realize small, gradual successes of letting go of control, they may become more open to change. This may be the best strategy for those who find themselves struggling under Muti types, and who can use gaps to educate their leader about the possible gains in change and growth. Of course, toppling the dictator is always an option, but revolutions carry their own price tags.

CHAPTER FIVE

The Godfather: Arturo Toscanini

Toscanini is to conducting what Einstein is to physics: the biggest brand name ever, synonymous with the name of the profession itself.

Born in the Italian city of Parma in 1867, Arturo Toscanini became the first international podium star, his fame growing with age: He conducted well into his mid-eighties. He was music director of La Scala, the Metropolitan Opera, the New York Philharmonic, and the all-star NBC Symphony Orchestra—created especially for him. This orchestra brought classical music via radio—later TV—to people across the United States who had never been to classical concerts. His name—and the legions of anecdotes about him—became a part of popular culture, far beyond the circle of highbrow connoisseurs. Yet he was a complex man, not easily understood, as the difference between his behavior in rehearsal and in performance indicates.

When he rehearsed the overture of Verdi's *La Traviata*, Toscanini's coarse voice sang along with the violins. He clearly wanted his musicians to "sing" too, to have that indispensable *sostenuto* (sustained) quality to their playing. He expected every second to be infused with maximum expression, bringing conductor and orchestra to unite in total commitment to the music. Suddenly something failed to please him. His gestures had signaled "faster" but the orchestra did not respond as one—the playing was not together. Toscanini shouted: "Look at me!" and then, almost immediately, exploded. *"Contrabassi!"* he screamed at the top of his lungs, singling out the offenders, "You lazy oxen! Faster, faster! Stop dragging, blah-blah-blah. (disgusted) Oh, *Madonna santissima!* (voice trembling with impatience) Faster!" Toscanini tantrums were famously spectacular. He was really losing it: swearing, screaming, calling names, breaking and throwing things, threatening to leave (and leaving)—all out of pure visible agony. The most frequent word in the stream of angry utterances was (in broken voice) *"vergogna!"*—shame. Who was being shamed? Mostly him. "I can never show my face in public after this," he would say, tragically, when some player disappointed him. At stake was the honor of the whole family, and Toscanini saw himself as the *padre di famiglia*.

A man of many gaps, Toscanini had a leadership style that was fashioned by the times he lived through—the era of great dictators—and yet he was an ardent fighter against fascism and oppression of any kind.

Players respected Toscanini and often feared him. They also loved him, perhaps because he was as harsh on himself as he was on them. He was devastated whenever he made a mistake—"I am *molto stupido!*"—in agonizing self-torture. Maybe because even when they were screamed at, it was never meant as a personal attack. He never tried to make people feel small—he was angry with them for not reaching their full potential. "I give everything I have!" he would shout, expecting them to do the same. His zero tolerance for a less than perfect contribution from his players implied a deep belief in their talents, coupled with his complete commitment to making it right. When he shouted, it was out of real pain for the broken music, which was their shared responsibility.

But even in music making there were two sides to Toscanini. Wild as he was in rehearsals, in concerts he was much more contained and restrained. Watching his face during a concert, one realizes how tense he is, extremely alert, almost worried. He is trusting yet concerned, a father watching his children perform a complicated, even somewhat dangerous task. You can feel his pride in them as they succeed. There is nothing about him that brings to mind an institutional superego waiting to punish those who are out of line (a notion closer, perhaps, to Muti's authoritarian control). That is why Toscanini's fatherly tantrums fill pages of musical anecdote books rather than triggering lawsuits concerning abusive behavior. (There was one exception: Toscanini angrily broke his wooden conducting baton and threw it into the orchestra, hitting one player on his head. The musician sued, but Toscanini was acquitted by the Italian court on grounds of "sacred rage.")

Toscanini grew up, so to speak, in an orchestra—he was a cellist in a touring opera company before he was called by his desperate colleagues to replace an incompetent conductor and save their livelihood and their South American tour. When we think of Toscanini's later relations with his orchestras, which to my mind are based on a familial model, it is worth remembering that he, as a child player and as a young person of nineteen, experienced the hardships of a dysfunctional family and was forced to assume the role of a "father." From then on, failing his "family" was not an option for Toscanini—and no amount of effort on his or their behalf was too much.

The paternal, protective leadership style can promote an atmosphere of trust, safety, and togetherness within an organization. Toscanini was strict, but fair. At rehearsals he was a disciplinarian to extremes but never capricious in his demands. He assumed the utmost attention and concentration from his musicians, and no disturbance or interruption was allowed. He matched this by being respectful of their efforts, being punctual to a fault, arriving fifteen minutes ahead of time, and never asking for special privileges of any kind.

The desire to perform well for the "father" is a powerful motivator, inspiring exceptional work. This lovely anecdote captures a beautiful moment: "The sharp rap of Toscanini's baton that cuts the ear like a whiplash brought the rehearsal of the NBC Symphony Orchestra to a sudden, shocking stop ... The men stared at their music, bowed their heads a little in anticipation of the storm. 'Play that again,' the maestro commanded William Bell, the bass tuba player, who had just finished a solo. On Mr. Bell's face there was an expression of mixed worry and wonderment. Mr. Toscanini noticed the troubled anxious look.

"No, no, no," he said, with that childlike smile of his that suffuses his whole face with an irresistible light. "There is nothing wrong. Play it again; please, play it again, just for me. It is so beautiful. I have never heard these solo passages played with such a lovely tone."

Lovely. But what happens when the father's identity

is so blurred with that of the family that his problems or shortcomings block their development or infringe on their rights? Another anecdote is disturbing for the lack of borderlines between himself, his real family, and his musical family. Toscanini, deeply dissatisfied with himself after what he regarded as a failed night in the opera, came home to his family, who were waiting to have a late dinner with him. At the sight of the set dining table he exploded: "What? After *that* performance? Oh, no, you're not. It shall never be said of my family that they could eat after such a horrible show!" All of them had to join in his self-punishment by going to bed without supper.

In most families shame and guilt play a certain role in imposing acceptable modes of behavior and group coherence. That role deepens in more traditional societies, where sources of authority tend to be ancient or timeless: spirits of ancestors, ancient traditions, or even a voice from above. Toscanini, I suspect, was not joking when he shouted at his players: "God tells me how the music should sound, but you stand in the way."

On the other hand, despite the possibility of such harsh intimacies, the family approach can provide employees with an overall sense of safety and well-being. That is why it became popular whenever business leaders felt threatened by outside influences. In a 2001 book, *The Corporation as Family*, Nikki Mandell reveals how, in a way, the Toscanini view of ensemble as family helped the bottom line:

"During the time of great union growth, large companies used familial techniques to protect their interests: improving workplace conditions, providing educational and social opportunities in order to keep the unions out." This widespread effort, she says, was based on the model of the Victorian family: The bosses were the fathers, female "welfare managers" were the mothers, and the workers were their children. There used to be a feeling on company floors that when business was threatened in some way, "the old man" would take care of it. The old man cares about the whole company, not just his fellow execs and top managers. He cares about the community as a whole too. His company, in his view, produces not only widgets but company picnics and other intimacies to show that, yes, though the boss wears tailored suits made in Milan, he can also put on madras shorts for a volleyball game with the third shift.

The late Harry Quadracci, founder of a large printing company in Milwaukee, Quad/Graphics, had a yearly ritual of staging scenes from Gilbert and Sullivan operettas (with new lyrics geared to his company and recent happenings) at employee events. He always took a leading role, and the rest of the featured characters were played by company managers forced to make asses of themselves in front of their employees and their spouses. This was, in part, to show that they were vulnerable humans too, in need of recognition and applause, even for lousy (actually hilariously lousy) performances. This served to break down the bureaucratic barriers—to show distinctly, with the exaggerated quality of stage lighting, that "we're all in this together."

The degree of success of such family-based culture will depend heavily on the personality of the key role player, the father (or mother) figure.

I was once introduced to the longtime president of a large family-owned company in the eastern United States. He told me about his first year in the job, taking over from his father, who had taken over from his father's father, the founder.

He was still in his twenties at the time and he was afraid of the employees' reaction to his lack of experience— so he decided to echo his great predecessors by shouting at everyone, just the way they did.

He overlooked the fact that his predecessors, not unlike Toscanini, were first and foremost appreciated for their commitment to their vision and their great know-how—so their rare tantrums were interpreted as a justified reaction to failing their high standards. In his case, every shred of goodwill the experienced employees might have felt toward a respectful, eager-to-learn youngster was destroyed by what they interpreted as an abusive management style. Luckily, he quickly learned from his mistakes. Now he still sees himself as a fatherly figure, but he treats his employees as autonomous, grown-up members of a family rather than as kids who have to be called to order. He says he is still "emotional," as he puts it, but professional attitude comes ahead of airing his feelings. When he does get angry, it is now taken as a sign of deep commitment. Besides, "emotional" can go both ways, and he gets equally excited and loud when moved by his people's success.

The line in bad temper that separates personal attack from professional attack can be a thin one. But worse, of course, is when it's very clear—temper is out of hand, personal, savage, and destructive. In 1987, well before Steve Jobs became a household name, the *New York Times* reported: "By the early '80s Mr. Jobs was widely hated at Apple. Senior management had to endure his temper tantrums. He created resentment among employees by turning some into stars and insulting others, often reducing them to tears. Mr. Jobs himself would frequently cry after fights with fellow executives."

This all sounded very familiar to me. I had shed a few tears myself in the effort to learn how to conduct an orchestra, a journey that threatened to tear down any sense of self-confidence, and that showed me exactly how the teacher or a leader should never act.

I studied conducting in Jerusalem with Maestro
Mendi Rodan, for many years the senior professor of orchestral conducting in Israel. Rodan was a no-nonsense
professional while I was a philosophy major from the Hebrew University with some training in music and the
worldview of a happy amateur. There was a gap there, and
Rodan wanted to close the gap the only way he knew. He
was the kind of leader who had to put you in his own mold
before you could be complimented or supported. I didn't
fit into that mold. Still, I studied with him until I earned
my master's degree in conducting. My thinking at the
time was that the more I suffered, the more I gained, and
that it was my fault for failing to please him. We became
close, in a weird way, like two wrestlers in the arena who
cannot let go of the other. Sometimes at the end of lessons
I was crying and he was crying. It was like a dysfunctional
family situation, because we couldn't cut it off. I couldn't
give him what he wanted, which was solid professionalism. He couldn't dismiss me as a waste of time, or maybe
he couldn't cope with admitting failure as a teacher. This
was the classic situation of the authoritative teacher measuring success only in terms of his personality. He was
ignorant of the individual learning needs of any particular
student, but knew exactly what "a graduate" had to know:
exactly the opposite of an "ignorant maestro," who knows
just what any individual student may need in order to find

his or her special way. Rodan could make you "a graduate" conductor, but he stood in the way of your emancipation as an artist-conductor.

Mendi Rodan was a fatherly figure and meant no harm. His passion for music and for teaching was, perhaps, no less authentic than Toscanini's. It is just that in the hands of a damaging authority figure, passion can be a terrible tool.

Can the idea of a family exist without blame or guilt? Anyway, the old family model has lost its viability in today's business world for many reasons, including the sheer size of organizations and the bureaucratic layers now existing between top bosses and workers—never mind the ever-expanding difference in pay—and later, the increased mobility of both managers and employees. Still, "We're all a big family here" is something one hears a lot. Is there hope for a genuine family-based culture, or is the concept—so intuitive, so powerful, so full of the promise of stability, acceptance, empathy, and caring—doomed to be reduced to a hollow recruiting slogan and an annual company picnic?

New potential for familial organizational culture might emerge from what is loosely called "the new family." In this more open concept of a family, a child, for example, might have any number of parents (usually one to four of any gender) and at least twice the number of grandparents, not to mention any imaginable constellation of siblings and relatives of all degrees. In matrix organizations, likewise, a software engineer can be a member of several teams of product development, each reporting to a different manager, while being on the payroll of a different department of the company altogether. It is clear that in these new structures the power of the "old" family concept will be loosened or shifted, along with some of the advantages of stability. However, the flexibility behind this new variety within the family concept can be of great advantage to new organizations wishing to retain a sense of family. The new family is no longer defined by a fixed set of roles and a set of personalities to match, but by types of relations that people choose to form within the organization. These relations are not imposed by the structure, but chosen for, and consciously drawing on, what people believe to be the best way to maintain long-term and meaningful relations.

How would a modern reincarnation of Toscanini, finding himself or herself leading a company modeled on "new" family, invest the emotional commitment of the original? In a new family-based culture, the leader does not impose his emotions on others, nor does he expect them to dutifully feel something in return. Instead, he has to make them choose such mutual relations, as autonomous members of his organization. A primary condition for this to happen is a sense of commitment beyond the purely professional sphere and beyond the everyday ups and downs of working relations.

Toscanini achieved this in the old family model by removing the borders between him and his real family and imposing the same pattern of relations on the orchestra. The new family model does not draw from the leader's family alone: Each of its members has to rely upon the full range of familial experience and filter elements from it into work life. Not all families are the same, happy or not, and the leader's role is to hold the space for the variety of life experiences to be crystallized into an organization's unique culture. This culture is bound to be in constant flux, constant examination. Its strength is dependent upon the authenticity of values, emotions, beliefs drawn from all stakeholders, so that "family" is not imposed but created.

Still, there will always remain a difference between real family and work family. But I don't think this gap necessarily weakens the argument for adopting the model. The way to make good use of a gap is not, as we know, to close it, or to pretend it never existed. The way of benefiting from that gap is through constant awareness and listening to the people around it. First, to ourselves, as individual members of an organization: What are my family values? And second: To what extent am I willing to carry them with me into the office? In my long list of values that constitute my understanding of family, I find that I am committed to helping my family create a living space that is beautiful, believing that attention to aesthetics is part of "the good life." Is that something I would commit to in the office? And of course this comes with a set of beliefs and practices concerning the way we decide at home what makes our place more beautiful—can I carry this way of negotiating, this openness to other people's opinions, into the office?

The manager's challenge is to engage everyone by exercising keynote listening beyond his personal state of mind and into the organization's sphere. He should ask himself: How open is my existing workplace culture to the main pillars of a family—that is, to stability, empathy, mutual support? It may be that the organizational space needs to be made to support these values better, by direct intervention of leadership. Familial qualities thrive on empathy and are vulnerable to criticism and cynicism. Even if not met with outright negativity, they are likely to die out before making an impact on the culture. It is a leadership challenge to listen and echo these contributions so that the process of absorbing and transforming these values can continue. This is where a modern-day Toscanini would put all her passion, along with her uncompromising decisiveness: in supporting this sometimes fragile and difficult process, exploring the gaps between different authentic family concepts, so that the family under her leadership could enjoy the benefits of authentic family culture. Moreover, constant dealing with the gap between real family and work family might provide another level of gain for those exploring it, as their learning is likely to affect their two families: It is easier to learn something new by looking at a distant mirror, from across a gap.

CHAPTER SIX

Play by the Book: Richard Strauss

In an age when politicians rise and fall based on their TV appearances, visual impression seems to be crucial. When I show Strauss conducting to my seminar audiences, they come to instant and almost unanimous conclusions about his leadership style. It makes them laugh. Very few would want him as a colleague, and the few who would take him as their boss can think of only one reason: He is so ineffective, they say, that they would be able to do whatever they wanted without him interfering in any way. So what do our eyes miss here? After all, Strauss's contemporaries famously claimed that he was a wonderful conductor, but there is no visual evidence to that whatsoever.

Richard Strauss (1864–1949) was certainly one of the towering figures of twentieth-century music, first and foremost as a composer, having created works that are still an essential part of the repertory of any respectable opera house. Works such as *Elektra* and *Salome* pushed the boundaries of the art form with new orchestral sound and other bold and unfamiliar aspects.

The composer/conductor's life, especially his later life, would make for a great opera itself, especially around his complicated relations with the Third Reich.

But if his life and his music were full of drama, his conducting wasn't. The film fragments we have—and we're lucky to have them, as they were recorded in early 1940, when the world was on fire—show him nearing his eighties. As the orchestra plays one of Strauss's own compositions, the conductor's low eyelids suggest a state of detachment, as if half asleep, only occasionally opening for a short, highly focused look in the direction of one of the sections of the orchestra.

The few gestures that stick out of the continual series of very small and almost monotonous hand movements are all of a reactive nature: Strauss is seemingly startled by a loud, booming timpani, and raises his left hand as if hushing another section of the orchestra.

Nothing in his conducting is proactive, anticipating action. He is only holding the orchestra back: "It's too much already" his gestures seem to say. "Get back inside the box!" Is Strauss's old age at the time of filming the reason for that complete lack of engagement and enthusiasm? Is it burnout or a leadership style?

The young Strauss himself gave us the answer to this question, writing what he called "The Ten Golden Rules for the Album of a Young Conductor." The list is written in his half-humorous style, and as is quite often the case with Strauss, one cannot be sure whether he is being serious or sarcastic—I suspect both at once. The list includes the simple rule: "Do not sweat!" as well as the somewhat perplexing instruction never to look at the trombones (and other brass), as "it only encourages them!"

Both rules taken together give us an interesting insight into his attitude both toward himself and toward his musicians. It is not about me, says Strauss: I am not giving a show here, or putting in the energy, or making any effort to become a source of inspiration for my players or my listeners. Hence I do not sweat. It's also not about you, who play the music. You should not bring in too much enthusiasm, or make an extra effort, or—God forbid—come up with a view or an idea that may require a change in how we do things.

What is it all about, then? The answer is made

visually clear by Strauss's conducting, as he is constantly turning pages of the score, even when they are playing his own music. It is clear that he doesn't need to be reminded of something he composed himself; he is looking at the written score to make sure everyone else understands where the source of authority is. It is all about the score, the written text. The subtext is also that the conductor himself is also under the authority of the written code (even if the code was written by him).

"Play by the book!" says the composer/conductor. No interpretation allowed—only execution is demanded. As conductor he is simply supervising the re-creation of what is already complete: in this case, his own written music.

Regarding his collaborators, the orchestra players, his way of accomplishing the task calls for a mixture of light-handed and trusting professionalism and glimpses of easygoing sarcasm. That is made possible by his careful a priori denial of the possibility of gaps. In the first place, there is no possibility of a gap between written music and its execution, because no interpretation is invited.

There are no personal gaps in the team, because the players are expected, as professionals, to leave their personal issues outside the door. Strauss himself displays the same detached, impersonal air.

He cleverly avoids gaps in control by practically

abolishing direct control. Displaying full trust in his men, he makes critical remarks only in reaction to mistakes. In this way, Strauss helps his men to a sense of self-confidence, coupled with a sense of self-control.

"Trust" is generally associated with lack of control, and therefore with freedom. Trusting is always a virtue, we're led to believe. But trust exists only within a certain context, certain boundaries. Strauss trusts his men to play by the rules, not to question them. If we dare look outside the musical context, to the circumstances of Strauss's life in Germany of the 1930s and '40s—what terrible times to trust people to follow rules and not question them.

However, even trust that is very narrow in scope—execution only—can create a positive response. The players felt professionally flattered, a feeling enhanced, of course, by Strauss's great reputation as a composer. Even his sarcastic dismissal of what he took to be out-of-line enthusiasm was tolerated by the musicians because he was no less sarcastic about himself: "I may not be a first-rate composer," he famously said, "but I am a first-class second-rate composer!" Again—no gaps: We are all mediocre, after all.

What kind of performance can Strauss create? Does the bureaucratic "follow the rules" paradigm coupled with personal detachment suck all the life out of his music making?

In truth, removing emotional indulgence in his

orchestral recordings served to expose structure—like modern architecture's avoidance of decoration in order to clarify the structural qualities of the building. Structure is an objective attribute of the piece, while emotion is more subjective and depends on the people involved. Strauss as a composer, especially when conducting his own music, wanted to defend it from being overinterpreted by the players. His success came at the price of the performances becoming detached, and the music's emotional potential is rarely fully realized. This is a possible learning point for the manager who, having "composed" his masterful work plans, now wishes to see them go through "unspoiled." There is a price for refusing interpretation. Appoint someone else for the execution phase: Your own ideas may be enriched by the interpretation of others.

The possible advantages of Strauss's style do not immediately meet the eye of the spectator, and even the interested listener could appreciate structure and consistency in retrospect only. That is probably the reason why the people of Goldman Sachs whom I met in New York—all of them keen on structure and consistency, and hardly suspected of being overemotional when it came to the proper application of their exacting financial expertise—well, even they couldn't dig him.

On that day, 356 newly promoted managing directors from around the world took the ferry across the

Hudson River from their Manhattan hotels to Goldman's conference center in Jersey City. It was a brutally cold day and the ferry required a little more time than customary. But for the new managing directors it was a minor inconvenience, as they had come from as far away as Hong Kong, Frankfurt, Tokyo, and London. I was invited to discuss leadership with them in the light of the new responsibilities they would now have.

I met with extremely intelligent people who were obviously very conscious of the importance of conforming to rules. I could have sensed that from the nature of our e-mailing and conference calls preceding the event, which was an unusually lengthy business. Everything that was proposed and agreed upon—even with keen enthusiasm— had to be double-checked and approved by more company officers. I noticed that my partners were careful not to let their personal passions or interests show up too much. Procedure had to come first.

The morning sessions of the day were devoted to intense discussions of company policy and ethics. Some of the presenters, according to views I gathered later from various participants, formed a respectable variety of Richard Strauss impersonators. These were straightforward, by-the-book presentations that made very clear how Goldman wants to do business in the twenty-first century.

A sense of order and precision was what I felt as I

walked into the GS conference center. Security was tight, and the day's schedule unbendable; everything ran right to the minute, and the whole shining building beamed with proud, hard-core corporate culture. Something, though, didn't quite fit in: me. "Are you going to wear these jeans?" asked a GS organizer in cautious disbelief—such an affront to the Goldman culture, apparently, had not been anticipated. To my relief, another organizer intervened: "That can save him some explaining on how different our working worlds are," he said. Now that there was a functional reason for my wearing jeans, we could all proceed.

When I took the podium, I looked out over a sea of dark blue, with some gray and black spots. Conversing with the men and women hidden behind the business uniform was my challenge. I had to start by breaking some more rules—not just for fun, but to open the necessary gap.

The first thing I accomplished at Goldman Sachs, however, was some furniture moving. When people sit around banquet tables, at least a third of them can't see the speaker without craning their necks. I asked people in those positions and some of those executives sitting in the back to pick up their chairs, leave their tables, and move close to the stage. "Please," I said. "It'll be easier for us to have a conversation, and it's our space—we can do what we want!" Still, nobody moved. There was, apparently, an unwritten law—follow the rules, stay inside the box. The box means sit where your name tag is. Finally, one adventurous fellow picked up his chair and walked toward me. Remarkably, no Goldman Sachs top boss stood up and said, "You're fired for violating the Chair Moving Rule." So others began to do the same, and soon there was an array of furniture near the podium, nice and cozy, and we could start the conversation.

This interior redecorating seemed to loosen up the crowd just a little bit as I began the seminar, inviting folks to weigh in whenever they wanted and explaining my view that we were all going to be ignorant together.

When I talked about pleasing their clients, they looked up from their coffees. This interested them. "Your clients," I said—"You still have a few clients, don't you?" There was laughter from a few. A few others looked around their tables as if to see whether it would be wise to stifle a basic emotion or to go with the flow. Little by little, as we engaged in some simple music making and started sharing thoughts about the various conductors I presented, the group loosened up and I heard some of the most insightful thinking I've come across in these discussions.

When playing the game of which conductor would you choose to be your boss, none of them invited the leadership style of Richard Strauss. "He's bored," came voices from the crowd. "He's looking forward to his pension." "No inspiration!" and more in the same spirit (but none quite matching my favorite, from a conference of hospital managers: "Was this clip taken before or after Strauss's death?"). In short, not one of the 356 people present wanted to be led by someone who plays by the book only. Neither, I should add, did the organizers of the two-day seminar at GS, and that is probably why they invited me. They knew that, as a classical musician, I do have my books to follow, but my success depended on seeing the book as a starting point, not as a mission accomplished.

As the hour and fifteen minutes I was allotted flew by, the organizers had a book of their own to follow. In the back of the banquet room I could see they were concerned about time. They held up signs. First, "15 minutes." Then, "5 minutes." I was reminded of the cymbal player at the back of the orchestra, who usually spends nearly the entire length of the piece just waiting—and when his big moment comes: *Bang!* and the job is done. Of course there is a difference: The cymbal player does not follow the clock, ticking mechanically, completely indifferent to the flow of the piece. In fact, he is actively listening to the music, so that his bang is—in timing and tone—the culmination of the piece. A bang at the wrong time would ruin the work of the entire orchestra. Our sign bearers, alas, followed the logic of the clock alone. That is why I had to ignore their messages—smiling apologetically—and go into overtime. Completing our joint thought process, I took it upon myself to decide, was more important to GS than getting to the scheduled group photograph and the evening's cocktails on time. I was glad to find that there was consent in the room, and later, approval from the organizers. They knew I was not disrespectful to the "book," and they understood my decision was in alignment with the understanding that had been reached in the seminar: The book is just the beginning.

I am reminded of one occasion where I was the one representing the book—against my will, and against the best interest of my project.

My Tel Aviv Symphony was engaged in what was in the eighties a popular trend: a joint concert with a leading rock group. The leading Israeli band of the time was Friends of Natasha. I loved their music, and I believed playing together would have an artistic added value beyond gimmick. Alas, I failed to anticipate practical implications of the gap between the symphony and the rock band. It was a disaster.

Symphony orchestras' rehearsal time is extremely expensive and therefore limited. Players' contracts mention the maximum rehearsal hours and number of concerts per month. The idea is to leave the player enough time to work and improve individually. This is not the work ethic of a rock band.

I met with the band a few times by myself to look at the music, and we were all quite excited about it. I made sure they all knew the rehearsing schedule: "See you tomorrow! We start at nine!" I said, and they all nodded. With rehearsal scheduled for 9 to 12, I was understandably quite upset when they arrived around 11. "You realize we have till noon only?"

They thought I was joking: "What do you mean till twelve? We're supposed to practice until we're all happy with the result!?" and of course they were absolutely right. But not for "the book" of the symphony orchestra. People had other obligations: kids to take from school, music lessons to teach—it was hopeless, and both sides felt disrespected. We somehow pulled out a functional rehearsal in the allocated time, but not happily.

I was musical director and there was nothing I could do: "The book" was stronger. I could find only partial comfort in knowing that other orchestras had the same rigid culture. I could remember the deep frustration I once felt during a rehearsal of the Israel Philharmonic. The aging Leonard Bernstein was conducting with great emotion and complete immersion, his eyes closed, the end of a Mahler symphony. He gave the cue for the last agonized cry of the horn section—and no horns sounded.

Startled, he opened his eyes to discover that the horn players had simply gone home. The time was 1:04 p.m., and the rehearsal officially ended at one.

So why do managers and employees alike, in so many instances, stick to a "by the book" approach even if they understand the inherent damage in being rigid about it? Why not, in a commonsense way, use the book as guideline only? I think the reason is fear—fear of the slippery slope. Once you allow a gap to open (between the book and its execution) you cannot control it anymore. Heresy, even to a small degree, leads to complete heresy. Employees, like orchestra musicians, are afraid of being exploited, and bosses, like Strauss, fear losing control. The book provides safety.

Alas, safety is not really safety. It can turn into a blockage of innovation that would have led to longer-term success and sustainability.

This complexity may be illustrated by the very successful company called Intel. The biggest in its field, Intel has about 82,500 employees in R&D, and manufactures microchips. Intel posts this mission statement: "Delight our customers, employees, and shareholders by relentlessly delivering the platform and technology advancements that become essential to the way we work and live." But the way toward "delight" doesn't come through easygoing laissez-faire reality.

I gave a presentation not long ago to young team leaders at Intel's Israeli manufacturing plant. As I began to play the videos, I noticed that one of the ceiling lights made it difficult to see the images on the screen. I stopped the presentation, got a chair, stood on the chair, and began to unscrew the lightbulb. To my great surprise, there was an outcry from those assembled: "You can't do this," they all shouted together, as if I had found the combination to the Intel corporate safe and removed all of the profits. "Other people in the company are in charge of lightbulbs!" A person can't go around and unscrew objects because there are rules about such things. There are rules about everything, I was told.

Why was I surprised? Because in Israel everyone feels that rules are important, but somehow the rules never apply to his particular case. Everyone should stand in a queue, but "I only have a short question—so I don't have to wait!" Or to a police officer while stopping in an illegal place, "I only stopped for a second to drop off my mother—she's eighty-two! I won't pay!" And then applying the same looseness to the laws of physics: "This appliance label says it is for indoor use only? But I can wrap it in plastic and use it outside—it hasn't rained a lot this winter." Naturally, every now and then something goes terribly wrong. This constant improvisation, the hacking of any system, also gave rise to "the start-up nation" (coined in the 2009 book by Dan Senor and Saul Singer). This is the culture Intel was facing when opening its R&D center in Israel—and of course creativity was a major resource, but it had to be restrained. In the Israeli Intel Fab—where chips are manufactured—and even in the conference rooms, in sharp contrast to the Israeli spirit, there was no room for improvisation, only for following rules.

Intel is very proud of its "disciplined engineers." What Intel seeks, according to company insiders, is "disciplined innovation"—innovation, but *only* according to the rules. The rules supposedly ensure compatibility with other groups working on the same product and with other Intel products.

One Intel manager told me of a guy on his team who had a brilliant idea for a new feature to be incorporated in the next generation of chips. This guy developed his idea according to the needs of, and in collaboration with, a customer. Unfortunately, he did not follow Intel rules, and because of that his program did not promise compatibility with other Intel customers' machines. Not only was the brilliant solution not incorporated into the next generation of Intel products, the company also lost crucial time until another solution could be developed "within the rules." In this case, it was undisciplined innovation that killed innovation, because the product never reached the customers.

Intel's clever solution to the problem was not to

write more rules encouraging engineers to follow the rules. Instead it created a new position of T Fellows, whose role in the system is not to manage other people but to manage ideas: to promote and harness free innovation, and see that it reaches Intel's products by complying with the rules. The Intel solution is beautiful because it holds the stick from both sides. Intel did not flex its book, but created an assisted channel for innovation so that the book will not hold back its inventive engineers.

So "book" is indispensable—in the case of Intel as it is in the case of Strauss.

However, strictly speaking there is no such thing as "playing by the book," since every book needs interpretation. In other words, interpretation is not a luxury indulged in by ego-driven individuals—it is an absolute necessity. There are very few cases where there is only one acceptable interpretation—as in an instruction page for IKEA's products. Even texts that are carefully constructed to avoid multiple interpretations, such as laws or regulations, often fail: The complexity of the real situation is too great. This is why we have law courts and symphony orchestras: to give interpretations to the complex plans. That is why we can see honorable judges disagree, and why it takes the Detroit Symphony only thirty-two minutes and forty seconds to play Beethoven's Fifth Symphony, but the Berlin Philharmonic takes nearly two minutes longer. And it is true that we consciously put ourselves on that slippery slope, in that opened gap, constantly having to rethink the validity of our interpretations. That, however, is far better than living in denial of the gap.

Everyday life teaches us that even running an errand to the supermarket at your spouse's request to "buy two yogurts" can be quite challenging once confronted with the many optional interpretations: Regular. Reduced fat. Low fat. No fat. Greek. American. French. How do you play by the book with your spouse's instructions when the book is full of paradoxes and competing theories? Lost for interpretation, you call your spouse. What a relief to be told! But what if you took a daring step and decided for yourself which yogurt to buy? There is some risk involved, but discovery always involves risk. Even if your organization is totally risk averse, the better way to reduce risk is through welcoming gaps—new interpretations—and creating a trustful atmosphere where everyone can share and try out fresh ideas. If these people fail, they fail fast and with no great cost. Even a Strauss-type leader is bound to realize the emergence of some good ideas through such a process, even if the chances are that he might have a hard time admitting it.

CHAPTER SEVEN

The Leader as Guru: Herbert von Karajan

They called him "the Emperor" in Berlin and Vienna, the two great European centers of the classical music he ruled for decades. For an unparalleled thirty-five-year tenure, Herbert von Karajan stood at the helm of the Berlin Philharmonic, arguably the best orchestra in the world. He sold 200 million recordings as conductor, more than any other classical musician in history—enough to make him the first maestro to own and pilot his own racing yacht and jet plane. He accomplished that by making the world a manifestation of his own ego. The world was his dream.

He stood erect on his podium, creating emotionally powerful music, and never even once opening his eyes to look at the musicians, who nicknamed him "the Magnet" or "Guru." A man of modest height, an extremely elegant posture, and a wonderfully dramatic hairdo, he was the centerpiece of the show, or better, the focus of a ritual. In his early black-and-white television appearances, Karajan (who insisted on controlling all aspects of any concert or recording) placed the players in semicircular ascending rows, as if they were the spectators in a Greek theater, while he occupied the place of performance.

During concerts, Karajan never busied himself with telling his players what he wanted them to do; he expected the players to intuit his every wish as if reading his mind, so that the orchestra became, in his view, "an extension of my arm." His head slightly bent toward the musicians, he listened intensively, highly concentrated. As his eyelids were almost always closed, it was his forehead that seemed to be the focal point, as if somehow his inner mental processes were playing out on his forehead, so that his musicians could read his mind.

Karajan's hand gestures were fundamentally different from those of most other conductors. The ordinary way of marking time starts from the top position and goes down, bouncing from the bottom point—like a Ping-Pong ball from the surface—thus clearly marking the beat. Karajan's gestures went the opposite way: They started at the bottom and drew the sound in upward movements—stirring up an opening, an undefined instead of a closing gesture. In many cases they turned into smooth, rounded, almost circular movements, leaving the players of the orchestra with no synchronizing signal. Normally the players would consider the lack of clear rhythmic signal a grave shortcoming on the part of any conductor, bound to confuse and lead to mistakes. In the case of Karajan, however, this gap created a fascinating group dynamic and worked to perfection.

But how? How would things work for a leader who does not define milestones, does not make sure the different departments in the company actually meet deadlines, and does not dictate the pulse of the business?

Imagine Karajan as the CEO of your firm. One thing you wouldn't get from him are memos full of bullet points for execution. If, say, he were sending a note to employees about the latest quarterly results, it might look like this:

"To Employees: The deep satisfaction of enhancing our earnings occupies my mind; moreover, the path toward greater earnings is well known to me—I embody the goal and the way of this company. Follow me, and our bottom line will

improve. There will be no discussion, nor any particular explanations given. I close my eyes and trust you to follow me. Come!

"*P.S. And don't forget: Grow your hair long enough so that it will shimmer in the spotlight, but not too much, because it is I who ultimately represent what our great company stands for, and we must avoid sending mixed messages to our clients.*"

Crazy, isn't it? Maybe not so much if we take Karajan's way of rehearsing into account. While Karajan's concerts gave rise to the guru image, they were based on detailed, even pedantic work in rehearsal, in which Karajan made sure by meticulous training that his musical ideas were perfectly understood and exercised, so the players guessing his mind in performance would not be in great danger of getting it wrong. Besides, there are aspects of the interpretation that his conducting conveyed at all times, such as guiding the musicians toward giving their sound a full and mellow texture—that sound was one of Karajan's trademarks. They said he could draw a lush, rich sound from every orchestra.

Still, what the musicians wouldn't get from him was the exact timing of the playing. If they were to look to Karajan for a clear timing indication, they would fail to get one. And since he did not offer this guidance, the musicians had to synchronize by themselves. The principal players (at the heads of the different sections) of the

orchestra had to look at each other (as if they were playing chamber music) and with swinging body movements,
actually conduct themselves and the rest of the orchestra.
The result is perfect coherence: thirty-five years under
Karajan as music director made the Berlin Philharmonic
play in perfect organic unity, like the inhaling and exhal-
ing of a giant live creature.

Karajan was often asked about his "unclear" conducting. Wouldn't it be simpler if he just gave the orchestra a
clear beat? His view was that the worst damage he could
do to his musicians was to give them a clear-cut instruction. That would ruin the ensemble because it would fix
the players' attention on him, disregarding other players,
and would get in the way of organic unity. Avoiding clarity
was how he made sure they listened to each other. That
was what made them an orchestra.

Karajan made his players accountable for their crit-
ically important "togetherness" in the same way the
string quartet playing for army generals near the Syrian border played together. Moreover, another level of
commitment is added by creating interdependence within
the group, beyond the one that exists between the boss
and the subordinate.

Karajan achieved that by applying a measure of letting go of his own control—in other words, by deliberately
opening a gap. How far was he willing to go with this

opening? In other words, was the gap a tool for better execution only, or was it wide enough to include the deeper level of interpretation? Karajan's ever-closed eyes served as a vital clue in answering this question, as this famous anecdote (among musicians, anyway) testifies: Karajan was conducting the Philharmonia Orchestra in London. At a certain point he cued a flute player for a solo, but the cue was completely ambiguous—a long horizontal movement of Karajan's hand, with nothing indicating "Now!" The bewildered player raised his hand: "With all due respect, Maestro, I don't understand: When would you like me to start?" to which Karajan promptly replied: "You start *when you can't stand it anymore.*"

What on earth did this reply mean? And what might it mean in other contexts that don't involve music making? Karajan could have said something like, "I'm not going to show you; I trust your professional judgment," or "Take it from your colleagues"—but he chose this enigmatic reply. What is the source of that tension or stress, assumed by Karajan, that a player couldn't, at a certain point, take anymore? Is it just the burden of his challenging task? Not likely, taking into account the fact that this person is a seasoned professional, playing in a top orchestra. As Karajan knew all too well, that stress was the result of a threatening gap the player was trapped in: a gap between responsibility and authority. On one hand the player was laden with the full responsibility of entering at the right moment, but on the other hand he had no authority to decide what that moment should be. Having to assume responsibility for something you cannot influence is a most unnerving situation for anyone, in any organization, and a manager who avoids dealing with that gap by discussing it openly is neglecting rather than empowering his subordinates. Karajan failed to address the gap, using its existence, instead, to put unproductive pressure on his subordinate player.

What, then, is the right balance between opening a space for inventiveness and clear-cut instruction? This is not, of course, a mathematical question, but one of interpretation, of trial and error, of an atmosphere of progressive and responsible ignorance and the welcoming of gaps. For a useful guideline we might consider the boss/employee relationship developed by the late artist Sol LeWitt, often labeled the Godfather of Conceptual Art. LeWitt hired crews of artists (in all, thousands were employed) to take his instructions—concepts that he devised in his studio in Connecticut—and then turn them into finished products. Like Karajan, he alone conceived the specific approach (he diagrammed the concept and wrote specific instructions). But unlike Karajan, he gave the artists who carried out his plans plenty of leeway, and trusted their judgment: There were times he did not even visit the site during work.

In this model, a Sol LeWitt wall drawing is a collaborative affair, one in which the leader depends on the follower to contribute a significant portion of what finally emerges. This, of course, requires not only trust but also an ability to communicate in a way that specifies the line between instruction and freedom to interpret—a line that if not well defined and observed can become fuzzy and a cause of dispute between bosses and underlings.

The plans for his drawings look mathematical and precise, leaving no room for error. But "error" is presumed and even appreciated—evidence that human beings, not machines, create a work of art, and one of the great qualities of human beings—even those who are highly trained—is that "perfection" is impossible. It's as if he were writing a musical score, knowing the orchestra will apply its own interpretation; this is not only acceptable but necessary to the finished product.

LeWitt, as is the case with other effective leaders, was more interested in overall effectiveness than in "the letter of the law" being carried out, and his ego was healthy enough, wise enough, to understand the increased value of collaboration—one of the assets that made him the most exhibited artist in the world, with more than five hundred solo shows during his lifetime.

Obviously in a creative enterprise—and all business and art qualify—communication, not avoidance, is needed if a leader wants to share authority, listen to other voices, and thus enable autonomy and emancipation. Had Karajan opened his eyes to look at the flutist in a way that said: "I am interested in what you have to say. I am listening to your mind, not only to my own mind's ideas executed by you. I'll follow *you* now," that would have been a liberating message, and not only to the flute player: Every other member of the orchestra would then have known that his time would come, and his voice—beyond the voice of his instrument—would be heard.

But of course that conductor who was a leader/follower would not be a Karajan. As Karajan did not open his eyes to look at the flutist, the only solution left for the player was to try to guess Karajan's mind. The true music, in Karajan's world, existed inside his own head: Everything outside it, including the whole orchestra and the sounds it made, was just an outside manifestation of the maestro's inner music. The world was his will.

In more ways than one, Karajan can be seen as a mirror image of Muti. Both are sole carriers of the vision for their organizations, but they impose their visions in almost opposite ways. Whereas, in performance, Muti strives for maximum control by clearly instructing each of his musicians, Karajan avoided clarity, expecting them to make up for the ambiguity—as individuals and as a group. Which of the two ways is more taxing on the nerves of the players is, I suppose, a matter of taste. I would prefer, from the point of view of keeping my mental health, to work with Muti, a straightforward guy: What you see is what you get. Which of the two methods brings better results? In general, my money here is on Karajan, due to the relative trust and space he creates by opening a gap of control (albeit much more limited than in the case of Sol LeWitt). I think you get more than what you see, that is, more than Karajan's own input. Which of the two is more sustainable as a culture of work? This is hard to say, because so many local factors of a specific orchestra come into play. History, however, is on the side of Karajan, who lasted thirty-five years as music director of one great orchestra, whereas Muti was shown the way out from his equally imperial position after only nineteen years. On second thought, it is not surprising that Karajan's manipulative control, in which the subordinates themselves become part of the control chain, is harder to rebel against, while the exposed direct control of Muti's authority is a more obvious target.

What happens in organizations when the true meaning of the work remains inside the head of only one person or a small number of people? What are the consequences of this top-down model, one that isn't transparent in its communication but leaves a lot to guesswork and speculation? What happens when ego trumps dialogue?

I was honored to have been invited, along with some three hundred other guests, to take part in the prestigious Forum d'Avignon, in the south of France. Over the last few years the president of the French republic, its prime minister, and the cultural minister of France have all been sharing their visions for European culture with innovators and stakeholders in culture from around the world. The idea of the forum is to promote culture not as a singular element in society but as an integral part of the politics and business of nations. This noble and challenging goal calls for cooperation across many gaps of interests, perspectives, and mentalities. Communication is the only tool with which these gaps could have been turned from obstacles to opportunities.

Imagine my amazement as I sat in the meetings, watching distinguished speakers—politicians and philosophers, artists and journalists—addressing important issues by dazzling themselves with their genuine wit and superb French rhetoric while the greater part of the audience busied itself staring into iPhones, or simply nodding off in the comfortable refuge of the high seats of the conclave room. The beautiful space in the ancient Papal Palace echoed with beautiful words, verbal fireworks that reached no one. Speakers forgot that speech is a form of a dialogue, a two-way activity, and that with no active participation on the part of the listeners, it is no more than a lost opportunity. To succeed in activating a dialogue, the keynote speaker has to become, at least to a degree, a keynote listener. Leaders who forget the necessity of connecting their own brilliance with the yearnings of their listeners risk alienating—or merely boring—the very people they seek to inspire and mobilize.

However, some speakers from the business world were less prone to fall into the trap of one-sided communication, perhaps because the habit and skill of keynote listening grows through experience in business negotiations. In general, people whose professional success depends on having an immediate, involved response from others in order to generate their own next utterance develop these listening skills. Stand-up comedians may be on the top of the list. Therapists and educators, and anyone enjoying the opportunity of direct, unmediated communication with collaborators, fall into this category. Senior leaders, detached by layers of hierarchy, as well as people whose communication depends on the written word, have to make a greater effort to develop their listening.

Many of us may privately aspire to be dazzling, charismatic, gurulike leaders; certainly this style worked beautifully for Karajan. But while we amuse ourselves with the imagined joys of shaping the world by the power of our personality alone, it is important to remember that Karajan's authority was based on real-world achievements that could be assessed by orchestra members, critics, audiences, and CD buyers all over the world. In that sense, there was transparency around his product. During rehearsals, preparing for the final product, Karajan's intentions were also spelled out and exercised by his musicians, so there was a balance between spiritual influence and down-to-earth training—and there were tangible outcomes.

But what happens when such balance is lost, when there is no transparency and no one can testify to a process, or even the validity of the product? Bernie Madoff comes to mind: a guru investor, producing beautiful music of 20 percent a year, each year. Nobody knew how, but everyone followed happily all the way to the tragic end, as the greatest Ponzi scheme in history robbed investors of more than $65 billion. Or Robert Maxwell, a kind of Herbert von Karajan of international corporations, a larger-than-life figure who, relying on force of personality and a great sense of authority, left others to guess at his intent and the details of his maneuvers. Maxwell's death in 1991 at sea in mysterious circumstances brought attention to the treacheries of his close-to-the-vest policies and the risk of blind followership.

The story resulted in a big change in corporate governance around the globe. Highly influenced by the Maxwell episode, a task force led by Sir Adrian Cadbury, the head of Cadbury and Schweppes, came up with what has been called the Cadbury Code of Corporate Governance, which still stands and which is intended to ensure proper governance of corporations—a spelling out of proper procedures for guarding against the power of outsized personalities and exposing important information to all stakeholders.

Fortunately, I never had the chance to defraud a large number of people and draw them into financial ruin, but I do have a story about arrogance and a Karajan-like behavior and its consequences that involved yours truly, and that to this day I find hard to accommodate. That is, what could I possibly have been thinking?

It was back in the first days of the new Tel Aviv Symphony Orchestra, and I, as the ensemble's music director and conductor, wanted to make a big splash. I just didn't plan it to be so big that it nearly drowned the whole orchestra, myself included.

My intent from the beginning was to provide something that I thought was missing in Israel's cultural scene—an orchestra that did not simply live in the past and play safe, traditional, and marketable pieces, as is, regrettably, the trademark of the nation's senior ensemble, the Israel Philharmonic. So for our gala concert

I included a Mozart piece and one of the less played symphonies of the Russian giant Prokofiev. Each presented a challenge to our audience, but the Prokofiev was not as challenging as my revolutionary way with Mozart. How could I revolutionize (and mess up) Mozart? With inspiration, adopting a Karajan-like disregard for how others might see it, this is how:

At some point during the rehearsals of Mozart's Twenty-fifth Symphony, I felt we needed to get the string players more engaged. Something was missing in their attitude, and it gave the playing a heavy, routine character. So I said, "Dear string players, could you please take your music with you, and find yourself suitable partners: We'll be forming as many string quartets as we can, on one stage!" So they rearranged themselves in small groups, with the wind instruments scattered in between. In this way, I thought, they'd be playing the piece as they would play chamber music, with more players taking charge. It worked very well in rehearsal, as the playing became engaged, albeit somewhat chaotic. It seemed so radically different and happily playful to me that I decided we were going to play like this in the concert. It would resonate, I reasoned, in a way that it never had before. Unfortunately, it did.

When the members of the audience walked into the hall on that gala night, expecting some semblance of order and familiarity, what they saw and heard was closer to a gypsy band gig than to a symphony concert. We didn't look like an orchestra or, alas, sound like one. Not only did the audience have no way of adopting my revolutionary perspective, as nothing was explained to them, but the players were completely out of their comfort zones and the effect on their playing was devastating. You see, if you're a violin player in the fourth row of your section, well cushioned inside your group of sixteen violins, you think, well, nobody sees just you or listens just to you. But with my arrangement, suddenly you're playing an exposed solo violin in a string quartet. You have to be a leader, to communicate with the other three players of your quartet. And with the other leaders of who knows how many quartets around you, desperately trying to keep together, and with the madcap conductor whom you feverishly hate for initiating this whole embarrassing business. The disaster was obvious to me and, unfortunately, also to the critics sitting in the concert hall. We were saved thanks to our Prokofiev, but the public damage was done.

What happened here? What did I do wrong? Was it in choosing to be inventive? Certainly not—being inventive was this orchestra's reason for being. Bluntly put, the problem was in my being a wannabe Karajan. Making people in the audience guess my meaning, assuming my authority and my ability to choose whatever I wanted without losing my following. Arrogantly, I just left it to them to try harder to get to the depth of my mind. I was the maestro, the guru, and therefore I could stay silent about my decisions: I didn't spend any time explaining my choice to my players—let alone consulting with them as to its wisdom and how they felt about it. Moreover, I forgot how meticulous Karajan was in preparing for his "magic" magnetism. If I had to do it again, I would probably triple the rehearsal time, and only then venture to present it in performance.

Likewise, I had neglected my audience's needs. I should have spoken to the audience first, and told them what they were about to witness was a musical experiment— made them feel they were in on something special, as if brought into a lab of music making, and asked them to judge whether it was a good idea. In this way, they would have had a stake in what happened, and they would have become, in effect, an extension of the ensemble they saw onstage.

The experience, whether musically successful or not, would still be interesting, challenging, and enriching for all. But, of course, to do that I would have had to be as unlike Karajan as possible. I would have had to admit that I am not a god who knows all. I would have had to say to the audience, "At the end of this, we'll take a vote; all in favor say, 'Aye,' all opposed say, 'Aw, take your new Mozart, Maestro, and shove it up your bassoon!'"

But can we envision a humble Karajan? In other words—was Karajan's lack of humility a vital component of his great success?

Let us ponder the seemingly unlikely success (and extensive admiring audience) of one such extremely humble character. To join him at work we'll have to get rid of our business suits and conductor's tails, and look for the thrift store around the corner, where we are likely to bump into one of the shop's frequent customers, the Peter Falk character Columbo.

You may remember the old television police series whose protagonist was a perfect example of the anti-Karajan figure—at least by his looks. Lieutenant Columbo's hair was not styled (to say the least), he wore a wrinkled and filthy raincoat, and the stub of a small cigar hung from his mouth—in short, he looked more like a homeless man than an emperor. As for his communication style, far from being a know-all guru, he gave the impression he knew very little, and asked questions that seemed quite simplistic. He would say things like, "I wonder . . ." and "I don't understand . . ." so many times that his opponent, the self-assured sophisticated criminal, sensing no danger at all, would gradually fill the gaps left by Columbo's seemingly half-witted questions.

And then, of course, came the final elegant blow: "Oh, um, one more thing," he would say, scratching his head just before letting himself out the door—and the last incriminating question was asked, the one that completed the found-out narrative of the crime.

Far from being simpleminded or forgetful, Columbo knows exactly what information he already has and how to get what is still out of his reach. He has full grasp of the details, in the same way Karajan nails the details in his rehearsals. Then they make a similar move: Columbo and Karajan both create collaborators (whether the musicians or the criminals) by opening gaps. Columbo does it by playing dumb, Karajan does it by being vague, and they both do it with great success. Karajan forces followers to be accountable for the details and to take ownership. Columbo outwits criminals into giving more information than they otherwise would have. In spite of the sharp contradiction in character, both display a magnetic quality of drawing the "opponent/partner" into making a move. In fact, the closest Karajan ever gets to pure Columbo style is when refraining from giving a clear rhythmic instruction, luring the players into making sense of the gap. As for audiences and popularity, lots of people fall for hero-type leaders such as Karajan, but even more people love and identify with underdogs, the "regular people" getting the upper hand. I think this is simply because we all have a story like that from our own experience, and we all cherish the memory of that sweet moment more than that of many moments in which our superiority was taken for granted. The later triumphal moments are the ones keeping us up at night, wondering if we are really deserving, or worse, when will they find out we're fake?

I'm not suggesting that rumpled raincoats become your dress policy, only that your success could rely, in part, on your choice to be vulnerable. By putting down your defensive walls of knowing all and handing over a measure of control to others, will you be able to do away with their own defenses made of comfortable routines, acquired cynicism, or—even worse—lies and bad intentions? To do that, you will have to play your own strengths as a leader, creating gap-opening communication in your own style.

CHAPTER EIGHT

Leadership Dance: Carlos Kleiber

This was a day to remember. A video clip of Carlos Kleiber conducting was playing in my workshop. As it ended, a woman said, with a wide smile: "Wow! This one is *dancing*!" Well, many people could see that, only this woman was blind. She could *hear* him dancing. Kleiber's rich body language translated into audible dance. He conducted with his whole body, using a huge range of movement, sweeping his long arms out, bending and swaying, grinning ecstatically, jumping in excitement. He could also be minimalistic, using only his fingertips or sometimes just leaning back, almost not moving, listening. His baton, a living entity in the hands of a master puppeteer, seemed to be dancing with him. In short, Kleiber was the master of movement and flow.

Kleiber's childlike exuberance and somewhat clownish grin could not have been more different from Muti's severe, dictatorial presence, and yet, surprisingly, even Muti hails him as the greatest of contemporary conductors. If you will, Carlos Kleiber, who died in 2004, remains the ultimate conductor's conductor.

Dance is only the second thing people usually notice about Carlos Kleiber. The first is joy—contagious, in-the-moment joy. Dance is his way to share and create joy: It is an invitation to join in a process of movement, in other words—in creating *form*.

Kleiber had a clear vision of the form, and so he led the movement, only he did it more like a tango dancer than a sergeant major. Where Muti keeps a tight hold on the reins, insisting on his own interpretation of every aspect of the music, Kleiber actually posed a challenge to his musicians, demanding their constant involvement in interpretation. He did that by using his power to open gaps. There were moments he stopped conducting altogether— simply stood still, listening—and others in which his gesture clearly pointed to the required effect—such as lightness or huge noise—without providing detailed guidance. His players, however, were not left in the dark, as these gaps were opened within a process whose logic they came to understand and share. Guided by the process (rather than falling back on a drill, like Karajan's players) they were able to create their own interpretation, in real time.

Kleiber modeled a uniquely liberating form of control by shifting from controlling people to controlling processes. Musicians were invited to engage in a process, which served as a basis for cooperation. They were granted autonomous space to interpret and innovate; in that sense they became *emancipated*. They were able to initiate, not just react. They were empowered to assume many more levels of responsibility than with any of the conductors previously discussed.

"Playing with Kleiber is like going on a roller coaster" was a typical observation among musicians, and I think that saying goes far beyond the motivation emerging from the high dose of fun and extreme challenge associated with a roller-coaster ride. First, the metaphor of a roller coaster represents a process—*movement guided by form*—whose logic is shared and understood by all participants. One immediate benefit for any organization where people are engaged in a process is that the fear of error, so stifling for Muti and therefore for his orchestra, is much reduced by the fact that many mistakes—but not all—no longer lead to an isolated dead end. A mistake that is dealt with as part of a dynamic continuum—a process—becomes a temporary deviation that can easily be amended, or even innovatively elaborated.

The roller-coaster metaphor also reflects two other aspects of the leader's role. The first is that of supplying the energy needed to start a process—always against gravity and friction. It is an effort of active will on behalf of the leader that overcomes inherent staleness. Mind you, that role does not become redundant even if the mission has already been rehearsed and executed countless times. If anything, routine makes friction even greater.

The second aspect is the importance of providing a safety net to those who may, at one point or another, lose their firm grip on the process and be in danger of falling out. A symphony orchestra—and the same holds for most organizations—doesn't have a steel structure on which the players are running their processes, as in the amusement park. It would be fair to say that the structure exists in the minds of the players only, before it becomes a reality in sound. In fact, these people are building a roller coaster while taking the ride. Another outcome of working without a totally solid structure is that the process itself changes each time it is performed. Being organically interconnected, all individual contributions mutually affect each other and turn deviations from the preconceived structure into opportunities for improvement and innovation. This means there is always a degree of freedom, of indeterminacy, in music making—and calls for an ignorant state of mind on behalf of all stakeholders. Clearly Kleiber's demands from the employees/players were far reaching, with no tolerance at all for those basically decent workers who just wished to be told what to do. With Kleiber you needed to think for yourself all the time or you lost your grip.

Such demands have to be rewarded, and Kleiber did so by constantly acknowledging his players' achievements. His appreciation was expressed through the joyful way he listened to them. Their playing visibly energized him, and this energy was transformed into his dance. Trust is another potent sign of recognition, and Kleiber showed his trust in his musicians by refraining from interfering in their efforts. Sometimes he stood completely still during the most complicated part of a piece, where perfect group synchronicity is required. Unlike most conductors, who think their active contribution during such challenging parts indispensable, Kleiber trusted his people enough to become a keynote listener: Silently (that is, standing still, no gestures) he listened to them listening to themselves. That created an enormous degree of concentration, and freed the players to listen to their colleagues. The result of this listening is better than what any keynote-speaker conductor-leader could achieve. This kind of mutual listening has to be cultivated.

In a rare clip documenting a rehearsal, Kleiber addresses the orchestra and says: "If there is one thing I can hear, it's whether the people playing are listening to each other." When the opportunity arises for individual recognition—as in the case of a solo part being played by an orchestra member—Kleiber becomes even more of a listener: completely present and involved, yet never instructive, his face projecting deep pride and satisfaction in a deserving contribution on the part of the player. Kleiber is not just listening to what has been played—he is also listening, in anticipation, to what is about to be played. In that he becomes a keynote listener, exercising influence through listening.

And this brings us to the broader issue of Kleiber's concept of control: What makes it unique, and how does it work?

From everyday life, we know that control of our physical environment is obtained by applying direct force to objects, in one way or another: We lift them, push them, operate all kinds of machines that help us apply the exact force where it is required, even give objects verbal instructions (if they happen to be equipped with Siri or the like).

Many instances of "direct control" are elaborate and sophisticated: A magnificent passing shot in a tennis game or the fingers of a violinist hitting all the right notes in a virtuoso Paganini piece are both highly admirable accomplishments of direct control. Direct control is tempting to apply to objects, because it is not supposed to contain any gaps—unless some part of the control chain breaks or malfunctions. Machines that contain an element that is not subject to the direct control of the operator are trickier to handle: think of a sailboat, for example—the wind itself represents a gap in control.

When people control other people by telling them what to do, they are actually using object control, ignoring the existence of an inherent gap: The person under control can always choose not to obey. This being the case, the necessary support measures—in the form of reward and punishment—are applied by all organizations, in different mixtures, in order to make sure object control is effective when applied to employees.

Muti supplied us with a good example of object control in music, from two complementary aspects. First, in regard to the music itself: He slices the continuum of the music into many short segments, controlling each of them with a specific instruction. When Muti senses a loss of control, he reacts by adding even more instructions, slicing the segments ever thinner. Muti also applies object control in regard to the musicians, moving them around with direct object control (without physical contact, of course). Kleiber's radically different approach derived from his concept of music as flow and his perception of his collaborators as human beings in flow.

Kleiber aimed at keeping the musical process in full flow, without losing any of its potential energy, and still under control. How can this be achieved? How would one control the flow of a wide river? There is no solid "object" to control, only constant change. Only once did I hear—probably from an engineer—the extreme idea "Freeze the river! Then you can cut the ice into blocks and have them under full control." What a wonderful reductio ad absurdum of the Muti way of thinking. But Kleiber chose a very different approach. The only way to exert influence on "water as process"—a river—is to change the terrain in which it is about to flow: build a dam or dig a canal. Make the uninterrupted flow of water move according to its own nature, but in a new path of your choice.

Like the flow of music they produce, Kleiber saw his players not as objects but as processes: When they play they are in constant flow. This is why each player in Kleiber's orchestra had, a priori, full autonomy and self-control, and was, consequently, engaged, responsible, listening, interpreting, and being acknowledged and proud in his work. Not only did the players enjoy a sphere of autonomous control, Kleiber himself was also in full control, not over his players but over the space into which they fed their individual contributions. That space, designed and characterized by the conductor, interacted with the sound produced by the players in continuous flow, to create music.

Kleiber used his body to portray the qualities of that space. He may have looked up to signify a certain "leap" and so invite and support a proportionate effort from a player who is about to "jump" to that height, or "hold" the sound in a way that implies heaviness, or mark a certain volume of space to summon a certain projection of sound. Kleiber also used verbal instruction—in rehearsal, obviously—for the same purpose, that is, to influence the perception of that space the player had to fill himself. Many conductors use metaphors to clarify the sound effect they want to achieve, but not all metaphors work the same way.

It doesn't go very far, however, if one says, "This should sound like the sun coming up in the morning." Even if the visual metaphor works, it only serves to reinforce what's already in the music—it doesn't open a gap. But this metaphor would, and on several levels: "This should sound like watching an eclipse through a blackened piece of glass." The weird quality, the contrasting mixture of dark and bright, the drama of your own curiosity versus risk of watching; that is powerful. Energy created by these gaps in the minds of the interpreting musicians can be harnessed and infused into the music making. For that, the metaphor has to fit with the participants. When Kleiber wanted his elderly all-male ensemble of the Vienna Phil-harmonic to "own" the music and bring out its sensuality, he evoked the image of a "beautiful woman, long legs, looking at us from above, but that only makes her more desirable," setting the mental stage for seduction, evoking a very personal mental disposition, a relation, and a sense of process in each individual.

To what degree is Kleiber's view of the process as key, the control of flow, along with his view on autono-mous co-workers, applicable in the real world, outside music?

I think of Kleiber whenever I visit the training courses of certain intelligence services. I am not at liberty to mention any specific names, for obvious reasons. Suf-fice it to say, these organizations are internationally known and respected as agencies that specialize in coun-terterrorism, intelligence gathering, and covert opera-tions. You might not think that espionage would involve collaborative improvisation—or could apply the other lessons of music making—but it's actually a vital part of the training. Field agents and their operators need to be able to adapt to every changing scenario, and do so while operating as a single organism. Function-based hierarchy, as opposed to a formal one, follows process, and not the other way around. That means that a junior agent in the field can override his commanding officer's orders simply because he has more relevant information in real time. Like a player in Kleiber's orchestra, this agent has to be equipped with a deeper understanding of the overall process, including training in different possible scenarios, so his autonomous decision making is coherent with the overall policy.

So if, as a leader in your company, you consider the stakes too high to trust significant autonomous input from your charges, it would be a good idea to consider this example of an organization, where the stakes—life and death—cannot be higher. Delegating, empowering, and emancipating employees actually enhance the chances of success in this most unpredictable and dangerous playing field. Yes, the boss is still responsible for outcomes, but so is everyone else. Ownership of failures and triumphs is shared by all.

More autonomy should not be granted to spies only. Even the well-known story of how Japanese automakers seized the marketplace, outperforming the complacent Big Three companies in Detroit, points to that. The American system at the time was based on a design in which hierarchy was crucial. Departments carried out their tasks, and quality-control staff members then checked their work. This was fine, but it created no urgent sense of responsibility at the lowest levels, especially when compared to the Japanese model.

Toyota, for example, spurned the top-down model and required every employee to be in charge of quality control, giving each one the power and responsibility to stop production if he or she thought something was wrong. Self-governing teams took great pride in day-to-day work and in outcomes. This was the determining factor in the Japanese achievement. And yet Detroit missed the point by ignoring process and the problems of classical hierarchy, and instead tried to match the results of their competitors merely by focusing on mechanical changes and advances. Without the changes in working relationships and in the sense of universal responsibility, there was no chance it could succeed at the same level as Toyota.

Specifically, this played out in the dramatic and tragic case of GM's eventual product recall because of a faulty ignition switch. By 2014, thirteen highway deaths had been attributed to this cause, and yet a company engineer had discovered the problem as early as 2001. That top managers didn't know about this major threat to quality control, reputation, and profitability until many years later demonstrates the difference between a process that encourages openness, allowing each voice to be heard, and one that relies on the rigidity of top-down procedures, and as a result fails to harness two of any organization's most important assets: the individual mind and the sense of integrity.

I have often heard the word "process" uttered with a light twitch of disgust by employees and managers alike. In a meeting with some very bright senior managers from one of the largest pharmaceutical companies in the world I heard the following account: "At Merck we speak about working in processes, but for us these processes are a nightmare. If a senior manager wants to change something he cannot just do it: To have an idea tried out one has to go through fifteen different bureaucratic stages." What they call process is really a series of milestones—similar to the way children's drawing books ask you to connect dots to make a full picture. But in such a case as Merck's, the heavy bureaucracy hindered innovation because it took so much energy to get various levels of approval that the wind is knocked out of the project and the people presenting it before they can reach the final level of decision making. The long-term damage is an attitude spreading among employees that positive change, initiated from below, is impossible. Federal government or state workers will find the Merck lament familiar. Indeed, the lack of a personal stake in improvement and change deadens a workforce, no matter how talented.

A system that requires various approvals from

above—while process is already in full swing—is bound to impede progress. Here you are trying to jump over a gap. You cannot stop in midair to assess what you're doing, but that's what management would have you do.

Breaking process into measurable milestones is popular due to the advantage of giving the management a sense of being in control, but that might result in the whole organization's shifting its attention to measuring and reporting, which in turn now becomes a cover-up—"We followed the procedure"—even when it is fairly obvious that the procedure is irrelevant. The original idea behind the process as a means to an end has been forgotten, and process has become an end in itself. Just listen to my friend Lary telling his real *Catch-22*–style behind-the-lines war story:

> In Vietnam I was a lieutenant in the U.S. Army in charge, for no excellent reason, of a food supply yard. I had to account for and distribute all manner of sustenance to about three hundred thousand soldiers—a huge operation. I had many Vietnamese workers in the yard, and the common knowledge was that they were stealing us blind. They worked for a couple of bucks a day and to supplement this meager income a few of them snuck cans, bottles, fruit, and anything

else they could to take home in their pockets. A process had to be developed to deal with this.

Some smart general in Saigon developed new forms for us to fill out on a daily, weekly, and monthly basis. In the middle of an unspeakable war came the birth, then, of the U.S. Army Pineapple and Banana Accounting System. Everyone's time—mine, the office staff, the general's staff in Saigon, and the general himself—was occupied counting watermelons.

In one of my last days as head of the food supply yard I had two visitors from the Army's criminal investigation unit. I was surprised to learn that while we were busy adding up Coca-Cola cans, a corrupt sergeant in charge of the food yard was loading trucks with cigarettes, candy, aspirin, and canned food and hauling them to town in the middle of the night to sell on the black market. Nobody knew about this, and the new accounting system couldn't track it. The Army ended up focusing its all-consuming processes in the wrong way and on the wrong thing—it was easier than looking for the right thing to do, which requires more curiosity and independence of thought—anything but a rote approach.

So process as defined only by procedure turns up empty and a waste of opportunity. It can't be imposed by a management in order to have control. It must be implemented in a way that draws on the wisdom and experience of everyone involved. It must be genuine, not rote or routine.

A true translation of Kleiber's legacy to business processes should have everyone on board from the very beginning—from the senior executives who make the decision to the people responsible for carrying it out. The process should be launched using the energies of all committed stakeholders, commitment that has been achieved through shared ownership. In Kleiber's work, shared ownership was achieved in rehearsals, while discussing the music in terms that called on each player to actively interpret and share; likewise, the discussions preceding the launch of a process in any organization ought to make as many voices heard. Again, leadership has to exercise keynote listening and ignorance, in order to avoid ignoring or denying gaps between different viewpoints.

After launch there has to be a constant process of sensitive fine-tuning by all parties in response to the gaps opening between plan and execution. These gaps are not necessarily negative; they may very well represent a call for improvement from any level of employee.

Rather than thinking in terms of achieving fixed

milestones (which might not be relevant anymore), think in terms of constant improvement. This of course requires heightened levels of information sharing while on the move, of real-time transparency, and of trust—these are hard to achieve, or even to recognize when they appear.

That's why Kleiber was such a glorious model for Merck seniors: They could experience the trust, the high-bar standard, and the delight on his face acknowledging we're all in this together. In any organization it is primarily the role of management to "beam up" these values, as Kleiber's face did. But there are smiles and there are smiles, and people know when they are being manipulated. Phony enthusiasm won't do. And there was nothing phony in Kleiber's joy. He felt it not only for himself but for his employees and his customers. Legislating joy is not practical. What is practical, and deadly, is relying on the wrong definition of process.

Let's look at the nature of some successful collaborative efforts, Kleiber style, including his practice of trusting his collaborators, engaging them by posing a challenge in the context of a process, and of opening space for autonomous contribution on behalf of everyone. Here is a tale of my own—involving a typically unruly audience—which demonstrates the good that can result when ownership is shared by all.

I was doing a series of introductions to classical music

for middle school and high school students: kids thirteen, fourteen, and fifteen years old—in other words, kids of the most challenging age, generally thought to be completely impossible to deal with in the context of classical music concerts. If you bring them an opera singer, God forbid, they fall over their feet laughing. They can't help it. So I had to figure out a way to get these students involved and prepare them to attend a full-length concert, part of a scheduled school field trip a few days later. I decided to meet all one thousand kids, in groups of two hundred.

I opened by telling them, "Listen, guys, I'm doing research on teaching styles. We're going to recruit a few new teachers to your school and today I need *experts*, people who have spent at least nine or ten years, five or six hours a day, sitting in a classroom watching teachers as they do what they do. Do you know anybody who qualifies?"

They were quick to understand that in this meeting they weren't a bunch of kids to be lectured but experts whose opinions were highly valued. They were not stupid: Had my criteria for expertise been fake, they would not have cooperated.

I asked the teachers to sit in the back row and not patrol the aisles. Any sporadic undisciplined behavior was taken care of by the kids themselves—they took it as a disturbance to them (not to the teacher) and got everyone to keep quiet. This was not an abdication of authority on my side: I was still there, supplying the platform and holding the space for discussion. But as I was honestly ignorant of their likes and dislikes, I could be truly appreciative and interested in every opinion they expressed. I found their responses thought-provoking: Some said that if there was a subject they disliked, such as algebra, but had to study because their prospective universities demanded it, then Muti would be their choice. In spite of themselves they'd have to learn. They weren't crazy about the idea of studying with a Muti, but they knew it was likely to have practical results. One said, "I'll have better marks under Muti, a better chance to get into college, but the minute the final exam is over, I'm going to burn every notebook and never give this subject a thought my whole life." Most of them agreed that if the subject to be studied was their choice for a profession, or would otherwise be a lifelong interest for them, they would choose to study with Kleiber.

A few days later, the same teenagers came to the concert hall for a concert by the Haifa Symphony, with me conducting. Again I asked the teachers not to walk the aisles to police the students, and they didn't need to. During the entire performance of the sixteen-minute-long, complicated first movement of Beethoven's *Eroica* symphony and the rest of the full program, there was no rowdiness, no laughter. The kids had been invited into a problem, their expertise was acknowledged, their contribution respected—to which they responded in similar ways.

And a final firsthand story about Kleiber-esque flow control as exercised in everyday circumstances. Notice how a slight change in the "mental terrain" can make a great difference in flow: For years I have been suffering from scooters buzzing through the crowds in the local park, endangering children and making terrible noise in what should be a quiet park district. For years I've been jumping at them, forcing them to stop, shouting and quarreling—I even got into a fistfight once—to no avail. They always had the upper hand, buzzing away and leaving me, frustrated, in a cloud of heavy gasoline exhaust.

One day I saw a rare policeman walking around the park—and just then came upon this ingenious idea: Whenever I see one of those motorcycles, I signal to them, a worried empathic smile on my face, and say: "There, behind the trees . . . police . . . I think they're looking for traffic offenders. . . ." First surprised, then extremely thankful, they flee out of the park. I did it hundreds of times—full success guaranteed. Look at the great result: People in the park are happy, free of danger. The ex-offender is also happy, because he knows he did the right thing by leaving the park, and feels great about learning a lesson without paying the price of actually being caught, and I am happy, because I did not act out of anger, but out of a friendly wish to help.

This tiny victory story is noteworthy precisely because it does not idealize the motivations of everyone involved. People did not change their behaviors because they suddenly saw the light and came to realize what is moral or beautiful: Everyone involved (including me) acted out of selfish interest, and yet the outcome was happy for all, and for the general good—a classic win-win. When you look at dancing Kleiber, his engaged musicians, and the delighted audience—and I bet we can add the dead composer's spirit to the happy lot—you realize that the true achievement of any collaborative effort lies in allowing a multitude of voices and interests to sound together, satisfying their individual needs, while practically—even if not always intentionally—supporting and enabling each other. This is also a supreme leadership achievement, for which Kleiber is ranked so high by so many.

CHAPTER NINE

In Search of Meaning: Leonard Bernstein

He was the one who in the middle of a performance put down his baton and kept conducting, or better, kept conversing with the orchestra using his face only: his eyes and eyebrows, his mouth, his nose, his forehead—all immersed in dialogue, delighting in the exchange. He's the one who went beyond the great power of "music as process," in search of music's meaning, and used this search as a drive for individual and group growth and emancipation. And, to me, he was the ultimate exemplar of a leader who not only changes an organization for the better but improves the quality of the work and the lives of those who work on its behalf.

Lenny Bernstein was the first orchestra conductor to enjoy the celebrity aura of a rock star, his public persona reaching far beyond classical concert halls (What other conductor would qualify for inclusion in Tom Wolfe's *Radical Chic*?) He was also a composer, a pianist, an educator—a genius in every one of these fields—and the greatest communicator of classical music ever. The first American-born, and the youngest, music director of the New York Philharmonic, Bernstein was a sensational conductor, but even if you never saw him in person leaping from the podium into the arms of the concertmaster, you probably could whistle his melodies as the composer of *West Side Story* and *On the Town*, hits on Broadway and in film, and as the one who made you understand Beethoven's Fifth Symphony in his televised *Young People's Concerts*.

I first met Leonard Bernstein on Bastille Day in 1987, not far from Paris. We students were gathered in the dining hall of a picturesque hotel, grand piano and all, where we were to sip our café au lait from large bowls every morning for the coming week, and we were all expecting the guest of honor: Lenny. That's what everyone called him. He was a bit drunk upon entering our student party; still he stood at attention, joining in with everyone singing "La Marseillaise" word for word. He did, however, dismiss the overenthusiastic patriotic tone by concluding the rendering of the national anthem by audibly uttering *tas de cochons!*—bunch of pigs.

Later he sat at the piano, never too far from his drink, playing jazz improvisations on French songs while in simultaneous conversation with all thirty people in the room, asking and answering a million questions. In short, we felt Dionysus himself had descended from some Olympian height to the American Conservatory of Fontainebleau, and we became part of his mythological entourage. Our weeklong conducting course with Bernstein was about to begin, and we were destined to take part in an unending feast of sensual delights, musical and human beauty, and personal growth. And yes—our conducting also got better, because we began to understand how to pour all that other stuff into our music making.

As Jonathan Cott, author of *Dinner with Lenny: The Last Long Interview with Leonard Bernstein*, puts it: "Unlike almost any other classical performer of recent times, Leonard Bernstein adamantly, and sometimes controversially, refused to compartmentalize and separate his emotional, intellectual, political, erotic and spiritual longings from the musical experience."

And what a breath of fresh air it was to the lot of us. In all our experiences as music students and assistant conductors, in our music-teaching positions and in our budding professional conducting careers, there were always large parts of our lives—our general knowledge, our tastes, our passions, our likes and dislikes, our social consciousness and political stances—that were not allowed into our work, for they were considered irrelevant or inappropriate. At the same time we were told that as artists we should go deep into ourselves in order to be able to connect with others. Something did not fit. It was like trying to dance without being allowed to use all of your body—as if being held on a leash. Now, with Lenny, the leash was off.

I need to be clear: Music was the focal point of our work, as this was a professional conducting course—and nothing wild or inappropriate took place. It was just that we were invited into music making as *complete human beings*. This invitation he extended not only to us, his students, but to everyone he spoke to or collaborated with, on- and offstage. Each member of his vast audience was included as they were watching and listening in the auditorium or even on TV.

Where Muti invites the participation of his players as tools or instruments, where Toscanini treated them as children under his patriarchal wings, where Strauss confined them to his play-by-the-book policy, where Karajan entrusted them with the execution of his vision and his alone, and even Kleiber invited primarily their collegial, professional collaboration, Bernstein summoned the whole person to join in the music making, playing, listening, composing, or conducting. This whole-person approach defined Lenny's main mode of communication: an all-encompassing dialogue comprising emotional, intellectual, musical, and even moral levels.

To engage in a dialogue one needs a committed "other side," and as Bernstein needed partners, he spared no effort in trying to get that partnership working. In one-on-one moments—even during the shortest of exchanges—you felt you had his fullest, unconditional attention. You were fully in the moment with him, and at that brief moment no one and nothing else mattered. The effect of such concentration is very powerful, even when short. An exchange of glances during rehearsal or performance was enough to create a two-way connection between player and conductor. His communication was completely personal and intimate. He really wanted to know about you, and he remembered what you shared with him. You felt you mattered to him far beyond your function: He cared about you as a friend would. This intimacy of his communication was not completely unknown to me as, during my teenage years, I used to sneak into Bernstein's rehearsals with the

Israel Philharmonic, so I had watched him many times from afar, half hidden in the darkened seats of Tel Aviv's Mann Auditorium.

At the beginning of the first rehearsal of each of his annual visits to the country, I witnessed the same extraordinary ritual: For a precious half hour or so he was not rehearsing at all but moving around among people, greeting each and every player by name, his arm around a shoulder, hugging some and kissing others. Engaged in a hundred conversations, he was catching up with domestic news, remembering names of children and events he had been told about maybe a year earlier. These were not just niceties but the manifestation of relations based on empathy and mutual trust. These precious thirty minutes were the basis for making music together.

Watching the performances that succeeded these rehearsals, I could follow their dialogue unfolding. I could see how Bernstein used his face and whole body to project an emotion or an idea, how this emotion translated into musical expression by the players, and how he in turn reacted to their playing—as if he fully surrendered himself to their influence. It consisted of a full cycle of communication, where talking and listening formed a two-way channel, almost simultaneously.

In later years I heard such testimonies from other orchestras too: "He reminded me why I wanted to become a musician . . . he gave me back my voice." I could understand this all too well, having conducted too many orchestras in which musicians gave up on self-expression and became tools of execution only—where their voices as individuals had disappeared, leaving the voice of their instruments to sound alone. The situation is easily translated into any profession in which the joy of discovery and creativity has been buried by routine, by expressed and implied limitations, by an articulation that life experience has no acceptable relationship to the workplace.

Persuading the player to take responsibility for his side of a dialogue was key for Bernstein in retrieving the human voice of the player, and for his self-expression to be legitimized. That may sound easy, but it is the hardest thing: You cannot force people into a dialogue—they need to want it. I saw Bernstein sweating over trying to lure players into dialogue who were just waiting for instructions, as if saying: "Why don't you just tell me what to do? I'm full of goodwill, I'll obey!" Bernstein would have replied, I imagine, by saying: "I cannot tell you how to play this oboe solo from the Brahms: I can only project my own feeling about it—'sweet!'—but then I need you to come with everything you know about sweetness—your love for your dog, your sweetest childhood memories—everything! And everything you know about Brahms and the right style, and about oboe playing. In short: Come with the whole package, your whole life, and tell me what *you* think about how this should sound. To that I can react. That is the dialogue we need to have."

Or consider a 1955 interview on the cultural television show, *Omnibus,* in which Bernstein said, "The conductor not only makes the orchestra play . . . he makes them want to play. . . . It's not so much imposing his will on them like a dictator; it's more like projecting his feelings around him so they will reach the last player in the second violin section. And when that happens—when a hundred players share the same feelings, exactly, simultaneously, responding as one to each rise and fall of the music, to each point of arrival and departure, to each little inner pulse—then there is a human identity of feeling that has no equal elsewhere. It is the closest thing I know to love itself."

In the center of Bernstein's dialogue stands *the meaning.* It answers the question: Why? Why should we play this music? Why should we listen to it? And taken into other professional fields: Why should we build this bridge, operate on this patient, fight this war?

The question "Why?" goes beyond the question "What?" as in "What are we doing?" That is usually answered by the existence of the institution itself (we are an orchestra, an army, a bank—so we play music, fight wars, make as much money as we can), and therefore is almost never really challenged. It also goes beyond the question

"How?" which is mostly raised in debates open for experts only: managers, strategists, professional musicians, civil engineers, MDs, or generals. Of course, in the age of "crowdsourcing" some input is gathered in new ways, but it still comes from self-appointed experts.

"Why?" is not about expertise. It is about the wholeness of human experience. It is about intentions and values, as well as ideas and emotions. In fact, everyone is an expert, so the conversation is all-inclusive.

Any dialogue is bound to expose some gaps between the viewpoints of different speakers. "What?" and "How?" dialogues tend to close the gaps and eliminate them in order to enable the group to act together effectively. Finally, there can be only one bridge built over the river that follows only one construction plan. A "why" dialogue, on the contrary, does not need to close the gaps by having only one "right" answer in order to enable collaboration. Diverse individual replies are a source of renewable energy for the group, as long as they can be shared and enrich the other members. One leadership challenge is to create the context for that exchange, the platform that should carry it, and to facilitate its execution with the hundred or so musicians of the orchestra. A leading metaphor, proposed by the conductor, is needed for the players to explore and make use of the gaps—like a temporary bridge from which one can look into a canyon.

But establishing meaning is not the end of it. It is a starting point, and in a kind of "reversed engineering," Bernstein's approach establishes processes and validates content. He claimed that once people have found meaning they can share, it is relatively easy for them to self-organize their processes, with minimal help from him.

Bernstein's insistence on individual players' having a voice of their own was central to his thinking—it is an ethical issue, but also an organizational necessity. It brings to mind "self-actualization" as defined by Abraham Maslow, the American psychologist, in his famous model of the hierarchy of needs. This model, mapping individual needs, has become widely known as Maslow's Pyramid. Its basic claim is that higher needs, such as the need to be loved and acknowledged, can be reached only if more basic needs, such as the needs for food and shelter, have already been fulfilled. "Self-actualization" was originally the highest level in Maslow's model, representing the highest achievement an individual could aspire to.

One possible criticism of Maslow's model would be the lack of inherent connectivity between "self-actualized" individuals—each of his fully satisfied individuals lives in a bubble. That did not seem right to Maslow himself, who in later years topped the pyramid with a new level, which he called "self-transcendence": the ability to connect to a higher, wider cause than your own self. Remember—and this is the genius of Maslow's model—that this level is achievable only if the person maintains his or her self-actualization. So rather than there being a trade-off between being a successful individual and being a member of society, these two positions actually depend on each other.

Bernstein aligns with Maslow in rejecting the false dichotomy between having an individual voice and being a team member. To become a team member in Bernstein's orchestra you need to have your own voice. You need to be emancipated. In musical terms: One needs to be a soloist to become an ensemble member.

The term "emancipation" implies an act of will on behalf of the individual, taking the responsibility for autonomous behavior. Emancipation is always self-emancipation: It cannot be granted—only taken. The leader—be it a manager, a teacher, or a conductor—should offer the incentive, support the will, and create opportunities for such individual acts of emancipation to take place.

When it comes to the organization as a whole, the emancipation of the entire group requires more than the emancipation of its individual members. It needs an underlying agreement on the reason for that group's existence—in short, a meaning beyond institution and process. In most organizations questions of meaning are very rarely discussed, because "they aren't practical" or "there are more pressing problems."

Moreover, it is generally believed at the senior levels that, for example, thinking about the meaning of capitalism is not relevant to a bank employee, or that the meaning of playing Wagner's music is not something an orchestra player should be busied with. Just let them do their jobs quietly and efficiently, without wasting their time on questions beyond their job's scope. This works, but only to a point. Bernstein's way of getting the organization to the next level maintains the exact opposite: Shared meaning, touching on the very fundamentals of the organization and its activity, created by inclusive dialogue—that is, employees as well as customers—is a necessary condition for group emancipation, which is needed for getting the full potential of the organization.

"Meaning" has always been acknowledged as a key motivational element: I love the story of a stranger walking up to two stone carvers sitting in an Italian piazza about a thousand years ago. He asks one of them, "What are you doing?" The puzzled carver says, "Clearly, I'm carving this stone," while to the same question the second carver proudly responds: "I'm building a cathedral. . . ." The story is moving because of the unperceived gap between the limited scope of his own job and the great complexity of the whole project; He is driven by powerful belief rather than by reason. Bernstein's dialogues, on the other hand, aim at achieving partnership through reason and understanding, as a way leading to a sense of shared belief.

Bernstein's dialogues with various orchestras assumed many forms—and each was different, according to the nature of the orchestra. Each dialogue addressed a different gap identified by Bernstein and was meant to draw maximum contribution from stakeholders on every level. One element was common: They were all conducted with deep keynote listening on Bernstein's part.

Consider Bernstein's first ever gig with the Vienna Philharmonic, in 1966. It was the first time he visited Vienna professionally, and he was about to take charge, if only for a guest performance, of the snobbiest orchestra in the world. It is the only orchestra in the world that only considers candidates for membership who have studied under one of the members of the ensemble for a few years, so they could "inherit" the Viennese DNA.

Bernstein had many credentials as a conductor and a composer, but he was also young, American, Jewish, and bisexual—attributes that, for various reasons, put him in a less than easy position there and then. Moreover, on the program was Mozart, which after all was home turf music for the Vienna players; American music, such as a Gershwin piece, would certainly better help Bernstein establish his authority. Bernstein realized the existence of a gap, and he could anticipate that, whatever his knowledge and triumphs in other places, he would face resistance during rehearsals for the upcoming concert.

So he set about to do what he always did best: reframe the gap. He started by reinventing himself as a fan of everything Viennese. He worked on his German, decorating it with a Viennese accent and characteristics—*Grüss Gott! Servus!* as hello, for one. Most of what he was about to say was memorized, a word missing here and there, but in a way that only emphasized his effort and motivation.

He left his usual radical chic wardrobe at home and instead wore an Austrian-cut jacket, a kind of national costume. At the first rehearsal, after hugging the concertmaster—Lenny was still Lenny—he humbly told the players (in his memorized German) how flattered he was to be there and how much he was looking forward to learning about Mozart's music from them: "I think it is my music, but it is still more your music"—so he was asking for their advice on the Viennese spirit and tradition. By the time he was finished with his introduction, it was clear how much he respected them, but it was equally clear that there was nothing more they could hold against him, as he acknowledged every one of his relevant disadvantages in the situation. In other words, he empowered and disarmed them at the same time. With everyone now smiling, he was ready to begin.

However, only a few seconds into the first movement, he urged them to play "lighter, lighter." The Vienna Philharmonic has a worldwide reputation for playing with elegant lightness, and it takes great pride in this—and it was on this soft point that Bernstein confronted them. So what was Bernstein doing? He had just given them enormous credit and now he was making it very clear that he was the boss, passing negative judgment on their level of playing. This abrupt change of tone on his behalf bewildered me as I watched that video clip for the first time. To put my discomforting question bluntly: Was this just a preplanned scam, intended to get the "opponent" off balance, and so gain points and authority? If so, the result was disappointing: a short-lived authority may have been gained, but at the price of losing long-term good relations.

Knowing Bernstein, I could only come to a different view. I think he made a genuine effort, out of true respect for the orchestra and its culture. His disappointment with their playing was also genuine, and the way he expressed it was absolutely in line with his idea of partnership and dialogue. His intent was to ask the players to be his equal partners. He needed them to live up to their end of the bargain so that together they might achieve something new. But he did this in a way that had them doing it before they knew it—by listening to their need for being recognized for what they are: probably the best Mozart orchestra in the world. In doing so, Bernstein was a keynote listener. If he had walked into the rehearsal in a more top-down way, bringing his own interpretation and not acknowledging the orchestra's great tradition, none of his finesse would have worked, even going to the trouble of studying the local dialect and dressing like a Viennese. If he had faked it—just presenting a few surface compliments—the players would have seen through the scam. His sincere efforts, to my mind, gained their respect, and so did his immediate demand to improve their playing. Was he less true to himself, dressed up as Viennese? I think he was himself in the way a great actor is manifesting himself playing the role of Hamlet or Iago. Authenticity does not need to be boring, and whatever routine you have, you still can—even should—reinvent yourself each time, because each time is indeed new, no matter how many times you've done it in the past: Be yourself, only reborn thanks to ignorance.

The realization that showing respect as a basis for a dialogue between equals does not stand in contradiction to the idea that maintaining a strong sense of authority is important to any business leader wishing to benefit from true partnership with co-workers. Key to combining the two successfully is the ability to listen to your partners, to their needs and expectations, and then mirror back to them all of their positive qualities as individuals and as a group, qualities that can best serve your joint efforts. This ensures that you will be complimenting them rather than flattering them. If your people can trust your compliments, they will also trust your criticism.

Compare, if you would, Bernstein's approach to leading the Vienna Philharmonic with the less thoughtful endeavors of myself, his student, in 1993, the year I was named music director of the new Tel Aviv Symphony. As you'll see, being exposed to the master, and being immersed in his ideas still left me with a lot to learn, because I hadn't yet made enough demands on myself.

Our home for the Tel Aviv Symphony was the Ohel Shem hall. It is in an old neighborhood, habitat of Bohemians and intellectuals—Tel Aviv's version of Greenwich Village. Ohel Shem itself had a history of triumph and neglect.

There, most of the great conductors of the twentieth century led the ensemble formed as the Palestine Philharmonic Orchestra that later became the Israel

Philharmonic. It was a great honor, of course, to work in this old building, where history spoke from every corner, even if it was so poorly maintained that the same toilet seat the great Toscanini once occupied had not been thoroughly cleaned since.

The Tel Aviv Symphony was not the country's elite ensemble, and wasn't formed to compete with the Israel Philharmonic. That organization had much greater resources and a pay scale that attracted the very top talent. However, we did have ambitious programming in the hall and outside of it. We often, for example, played outdoor concerts in poor neighborhoods to attract young people to music that they might never hear otherwise.

The orchestra was composed of a mix of young Israeli-born musicians, and a large number of immigrants from the former Soviet Union, as this was the time of the great immigration wave that brought a great deal of musical talent into the country.

There was so much immigrant talent that this joke circulated: When immigrants from the Soviet Union walk down the airplane ramp, how can you tell which are the pianists? Answer: The ones not carrying a violin case.

But if music is the universal language, Russian isn't. Hebrew is my native tongue, and by mixing it with a bit of Italian, English, and some German words, I did my best to communicate from the podium. During one early rehearsal the depth of the communication gap became clear, and it was not about understanding the words. We were going over a Mendelssohn overture and it somehow got worse and worse as we practiced. I stopped. "Something is wrong," I said to the musicians. "I'm not sure what it is. Do you think it's the tempo or the phrasing or something else?—Is there something I can do to help?" There was dead silence in the hall. After an eternity, one of the older players, a man of perhaps seventy in his very tidy polyester Russian-tailored suit, stood up and spoke. Compensating for his broken Hebrew with determined hand gestures, he said: "Where we come from"—pointing with his right thumb behind him, toward the east—"the conductor didn't have to ask what to do. He *knew* what to do." And then he just sat down.

The man wasn't being sarcastic. He was genuinely and deeply insulted because he was now working for an idiot who wasn't competent to lead—that is, who didn't know he was supposed to have superior knowledge, always. And I thought I was honoring my players by sharing my thoughts, even doubts, and trusting them to be helpful. I was ignoring a deep cultural gap, hoping that seventy years of Soviet mentality could be overcome with a nice smile and a plea for empathy. I was simply not listening to my players, and once they spoke their mind, I panicked.

Unlike my mentor, I failed to anticipate the problem and prepare myself for it the way he did. He didn't wait until he stood at the podium to think of what to do. He thought through the problem he was facing in Vienna, and I should have followed his example. It was certainly no secret kept from me that many of my own musicians could not speak my language and would not know Israeli customs. I had assumed I could do whatever was necessary from the podium—that I was smart enough and well enough trained to impress my own values upon my players. I had learned from Bernstein the importance of giving all of the players not only a voice but the absolute right to bring their total life experience to their performance. But I hadn't anticipated that life experience. I had displayed a certain arrogance.

Had I brought an outside context that resonated with them, and showed empathy and understanding for their need for authority, I could have used the gap to start changing that culture. I could have told them, for one, about my own experience in authoritarian culture, while in the army, and how the combat situations affect my view of the role of authority. That is, if authority disappears for some reason—say, chaos in battle, when no one knows where their commanding officers are—the troops have to know what to do, how to make new decisions independently. Besides, a conductor, an officer, or any kind of leader can admit he or she has lost the right path without losing face. The other option, that of covering up your own inevitable mistakes and blaming them on your men would be much worse. I might have said, "You're waiting for authority. Do you believe authority is always right? If not, wouldn't it be better if authority would listen to the people?" That might have started a dialogue. To do it, though, I had to be willing to take a risk, to be open to criticism not only about the tempo of a certain passage but also about my leadership in general. That takes guts. There would have been a confrontational element in what I could have said or heard in return, but that's not necessarily a bad thing. The result is that it's not the sound of violin players or violin technicians I was seeking, but that of artists playing violins—and all other instruments—who bring their total life experience and wits to the new moment, and feel as if they make a difference.

Reality taught me that success in engaging my people in constructive dialogue could never be complete. Protestors and naysayers are, alas, part of every group. Music is an egotistical business, and with the gift of talent also comes a tendency toward expanded egos and for the willingness to express objection, sometimes in ways that make you doubt whether you can get through at all. The only way I have found effective is to focus on the positive contributors, trying to overwhelm negative tendencies. Trying to lure burned-out, cynical players into cooperation and dialogue is not an easy business, and it requires constant listening and trying relentlessly innovative approaches, catering to conflicting needs and motivations in the group.

Bernstein's dialogues were all unique in the ways they unfolded, so very different conversations could result from the same leadership approach. An international youth orchestra, gathered for a few weeks for a summer festival, is a very different organization from the Vienna Philharmonic, and so are the needs of its players.

Bernstein was rehearsing Berlioz's *Romeo and Juliet* with the Schleswig-Holstein Festival Orchestra, composed of young people aged sixteen to twenty-four, eager for the maestro's word. He worked them hard, making sure they could deliver professional-level execution of the complicated individual and section parts, but when it was time to make music, he didn't tell them what to do. Instead, he became willfully ignorant.

He said, "Romeo and Juliet are sixteen years old—so if this orchestra can't get it—I don't know which orchestra will . . . certainly not the Hamburg Philharmonie, or the Boston Symphony. . . ." (All giggling.) In other words, take it away, kids. Lead the way by connecting to who you are: not a shaky group of inexperienced orchestral players, but vibrant reincarnations of Romeo and Juliet. These players could feel, just by being who they were, how every stimulus in youth can be outsized and exaggerated. Every look by a boyfriend or potential girlfriend is interpreted as the most meaningful event of the day, and each kid in that orchestra knew that in a way no old-timer could. In this way Bernstein gave them an opportunity for emancipation. He played to their strengths—their understanding of a kind of youthful all-consuming obsession—to get them to play in their own voices, going beyond where he was. He gave them the platform for creating meaning, but they had to make it their own. Yes, notes mattered. And accents. And tempo. And playing on time. But all those things were pointless without meaning. And the orchestra had to identify with the meaning so that it could be projected to the audience.

You feel this intensely every time you walk into a shop and talk to the attendant or deal with the hostess at a restaurant. You feel whether she is just doing her job or is genuinely interested in your well-being as a customer, so she won't let you buy the wrong product or order too much food because you do not fully understand the menu. But shop attendants, restaurant hostesses, and orchestral players can't just be told to do that. They must be immersed in that "whole person" approach that Bernstein and other whole-person leaders demonstrate. Naturally, in a business context there will be narrower boundaries to intimacy, and "the whole-person approach" should not be forced on people who just want to buy a carton of milk and go home. But this approach, if offered and favorably responded to, can elevate human relations as well as business relations to a new level.

How to bring about such immersion was beautifully demonstrated by Bernstein while rehearsing with a young international orchestra for a concert tour, playing Igor Stravinsky's *Rite of Spring*. This piece of ballet music is already a hundred years old but still surprisingly modern and challenging for any professional ensemble.

At one point during the rehearsal Bernstein stopped the music by waving his hands, and said to the young players: *"I think you're all too well mannered. You've been brought up too well."* He introduces his criticism, clearly, in the gentlest of ways. He makes his charges smile, open for change, rather than cautious and defensive in the face of criticism. *"This is beastly music,"* he said, *"brought to the highest, most refined point."* Bernstein exposes the essential gap of the piece for them to dive into: how to be wildly refined, or refinely wild. They are now partners in the search—but as they need encouragement to go wild, he demonstrates: *"UNNNHHCH."* He says, *"Primeval, primordial, or whatever you want to call it."* Bernstein senses that the framework for shared meaning is still too abstract, and searches for the right metaphor to enrich it. One feels he did not prepare his metaphors in advance, and it serves to further open the conversation. *"These are big prehistoric memories of Russia . . . or of the animal kingdom—a rhinoceros or buffalo—or like the feeling that one has in the spring sometimes, of wanting to be immersed in the earth itself."*

Notice the evolution of his metaphors: from historical, intellectual, and remote to the animal world, something you can experience as an observer, and finally to an intimate feeling everyone has had at one time or another. The seventy-year-old maestro found the ground for an eye-level dialogue with his youthful players.

"These dances are performed by adolescents, so you know what it's all about"—again, he is taking their youth and turning it into an advantage, rather than a shortcoming of inexperience. He leaves a gap opened, between him and them—he does not presume to know what they do. *"You're lying near a tree trunk and you simply want to embrace it— uuuuhhhmm. . . . That's what this downbeat is!"* The players look at Bernstein, and they believe him—that he is actually there, in the intensified reality he describes to them. More than that, they believe they can be there too. It is his authenticity, his openness, that serves as the fuel with which they can perform the leap of faith, to get into this mental place where you hug trees, and play from that place. *"Too much talk,"* says the maestro, more to himself, and

now this entire search for meaning and fully buying into it is to reveal itself in music.

It is no coincidence that the above stories were documented in the context of young orchestras, while the more difficult situation in Vienna occurred in a professional context. The fixed routines and the financial stress that make up professional life make breakthrough moments more rare—but even more highly appreciated by musicians and audiences.

One such extraordinary moment of transformation through reframing a gap, turning a possible embarrassment into a wonderful gain for all involved, shows Bernstein's mastery of ignorance, gaps, and keynote listening. In April 1962, during Bernstein's tenure as music director of the New York Philharmonic, he invited Glenn Gould to play the solo in Brahms's D-Minor Concerto for piano and orchestra. Gould, a native of Canada, had by then achieved an outsized reputation as a revolutionary interpreter, mainly of the works of J. S. Bach, but Brahms, too, did not escape Gould's revolution. A deeply intellectual interpreter, Gould held high his personal and professional ethical principles: "The purpose of art," he would write in *The Glenn Gould Reader*, "is not the release of a momentary ejection of adrenaline but is, rather, the gradual, lifelong construction of a state of wonder and serenity." Of these two words, "serenity" was in short supply that night, but wonder was abundant. For a concerto to be performed, the two leaders of the event—the conductor and the soloist—have to agree on the interpretation. Gould and Bernstein failed to agree.

The second half of the evening was the time for the concerto. Lights went down, and Bernstein, alone, to the accompaniment of applause, walked out onto the stage. Usually the conductor and the soloist walk out together, but Gould was missing from the tandem, so it was clear there was something wrong. When the applause died down, Bernstein demonstrated in the most gifted way I can imagine how to address a gap, indulge in ignorance (and explanation), and turn the whole audience into keynote listeners, making the performance an all-inclusive once-in-a-lifetime experience for all.

Since the reader is well versed in Bernstein-isms by now, I will trust you with the whole transcription of Bernstein's talk, unedited.

"Don't be frightened," he said. "Mr. Gould is here, and will appear in a moment. I am not, as you know, in the habit of speaking on any concert . . . but a curious situation has arisen which merits, I think, a word or two. You are about to hear a rather, shall we say, unorthodox performance of the Brahms D-Minor Concerto, a performance distinctly different from any I've ever heard, or even dreamt of, for that matter, in its remarkably broad tempi and its frequent departures from Brahms's dynamic indications. I cannot say I am in total agreement with Mr. Gould's conception, and this raises the interesting question: What am I doing conducting it? I'm conducting it because Mr. Gould is so valid and serious an artist that I must take seriously anything he conceives in good faith. And his conception is interesting enough so that I feel you should hear it too. But the age-old question still remains. In a concerto, who is the boss, the soloist or the conductor? The answer is, of course, sometimes one, sometimes the other, depending on the people involved, but almost always the two manage to get together, by persuasion or charm or even threats, to achieve a unified performance. I have only once before in my life had to submit to a soloist's wholly new and incompatible concept, and that was the last time I accompanied Mr. Gould [loud laughter from audience]. But this time the discrepancies between our views are so great that I feel I must make this small disclaimer. So why, to repeat the question, am I conducting it? Why do I not make a minor scandal, get a substitute soloist, or let an assistant conduct it? Because I am fascinated, glad to have the chance for a new look at this much-played work. Because what's more, there are moments in Mr. Gould's performance that emerge with astonishing freshness and conviction. Thirdly, because we can all learn something from this extraordinary artist who is a thinking performer. And finally, because there is in music what Dmitri Mitropoulos used to call the 'sportive element': that factor of curiosity, adventure, experiment. And I can assure you that it has been an adventure this week, collaborating with Mr. Gould on this Brahms concerto, and it's in this spirit of adventure that we now present it to you."

If the performance had gone off without explanation, some in the audience would have scratched their heads. "Well, an off night for a great orchestra, a great soloist, a great conductor. They're only human—mediocre happens." Instead, Bernstein brought the audience into the act to play a vital part, reframing a failed attempt to achieve coherence as a grand-scale experiment, a catalyst for engaged and informed listening. To sit in on what Gould wanted to express—that glorious sense of adventure that had no guaranteed way of turning out—was to be part of musical history being made, far from merely sitting through the 8,417th time, perhaps, a major orchestra and a famous soloist play this Brahms work. So you know it's up to you to become an ignorant listener, and ask yourself: What will I make of it? What new musical horizons open up? How will this new experience refresh my older Brahms experiences?

"It is not our differences that divide us," wrote the

social activist Audre Lorde in *Our Dead Behind Us.* "It is our inability to recognize, accept, and celebrate those differences."

The scope and diversity of Bernstein's dialogues speak clearly of the core beliefs that underlie them, as much as they speak about his constant search for the right solution in any given situation. In other words, there is no formula, only tentative answers to new questions that are emerging with each specific situation: How to cede power while also retaining influence? How to reframe a difficult situation so it becomes an opportunity? How to identify and use gaps to create organizational energy? At what point should you choose ignorance so that it opens up unforetold opportunity? How to come out at the end of a dialogue, abandoning your own idea without beginning to question your own authority? How to make other people listen? How to let go, without losing control?

Bernstein's legacy is made of these questions as much as it is made from the answers he gave them. Listen, for each new encounter will grow its own new solution. Each gap will create a new dialogue that will take you to new understanding. Don't be afraid of the new, even the incompatible new. Don't be afraid to give yourself in full, and to fully accept others. Don't be afraid to trust in others, just as you let others trust in you.

But be careful here. I hope you've learned by now that the merits of these great leaders are to be copied not literally but figuratively. You must adopt and develop what is genuine to you. Faking it is not a good idea: There is no secondhand authenticity.

At the end of the course in Fontainebleau, three of us were chosen by Bernstein to perform—sharing a concert with him—in Paris. When I was finally conducting Prokofiev's *Classical Symphony* in rehearsal with the Orchestre de Paris, I was naturally nervous. Unfocused, I screwed up a rehearsal—I simply couldn't bring myself to be there in full. The next day we rehearsed again, and this time it went much better. I went to Lenny and said, "You see, Maestro, it's all here," as I pointed to my head. He said, "Are you kidding?" and he pointed to his heart and belly. I understood it as saying: Generosity, guts, and love. When you love something, and you are able to give it away, it will come back in abundance.

Optimistic Coda: What Now?

If you were to ask me exactly that—What now?—just as we hear together the fading sound of the final chord of some really good piece of music such as a symphony by Beethoven or a piece by Art Blakey's Jazz Messengers, I wouldn't know how to reply.

You see, music doesn't call for a concrete action. It doesn't send you to burn city hall or make you quit your job. Instead, it keeps resonating in your head; your fingers continue tapping the rhythm. A melody is stuck in your mind, playing again and again. This resonance does change you in subtle, deep ways. It may also change the person sitting next to you—but in all probability, it will do so in a different manner. He or she will remember different motifs and synchronize with different pulses, simply because the music arrives on different grounds, influenced by their life experiences, tastes, and ideas. There is not a single change everyone has to go through listening to music—unless the music is really shallow and manipulative, enslaved to a text, like an advertising jingle that aims at making everyone buy the same thing.

This is why I hope this book keeps resonating in your mind. This is why it doesn't contain instructions on "what to do next." Rather than seeing this reality as some kind of shortcoming, think of it instead as an opportunity for you to shape a leadership style unlike anyone else who reads this book. You are unique in qualities and aspirations, in who you are and how you wish to change, and there is no singular formula you should follow.

That said, I can still offer some advice on the ways this book might help you change yourself, or the ways you may venture, inspired by something in the book, to help change your own professional reality and that of your organization.

So what can you listen to, on your way to becoming the best leader you can be?

The first thing is to listen to change, inside and outside. There is already plenty to listen to, since people are changing all the time and organizations are changing all the time. Not changing is an illusion (sold by anti-aging cosmetics illusionists, among others). We cannot avoid change, however we may feel about it.

So if you listen to yourself changing, and you listen to people around you changing, you start listening to people as processes. Remember: The fewer solid objects you see around you and the more processes, the more possibilities you have. Your thinking and communication will turn toward the future. That should bring you closer to becoming a keynote listener, like Kleiber. And like him, you are not a mere listener to change, as you are able to influence its flow—in other words, shape the way you change.

You must have been able to identify parts of your own style of leadership echoing in the style of one or more of the six conductors you have read about—maybe even in all six. I think seeing your reflection in multiple mirrors can be a great blessing, in spite of the inconvenience of not having a straightforward answer to "Who am I?" In fact, the best advice I could give anyone who considers a personal change is to start by thinking in terms of expansion and inclusion, rather than in terms of eliminating or giving up something of themselves. I believe this inclusive approach to be much less threatening to the integrity of one's self-image, and therefore helpful in sustaining the change. In other words, don't try to stop being the leader you are—rather, seek to expand your leadership perspective, to include the most flexible and diverse leadership solutions. I think this approach should draw you nearer to Bernstein and Kleiber, as they are truly multidimensional, each in his own style. The other conductors are great, if somewhat narrower in their leadership perspective. Don't give up your part that is like any of them (that may be what made you success-ful so far!), but create a wider spectrum for it. Remem-ber: It is all right to have Muti moments when you are a Bernstein. It is a pity not to have any Bernstein moments because you stick exclusively to your Muti style.

So much for changing your own mind-set—but how will this change manifest itself in the real world, where you are leading and led by others? I believe it is very much worth knowing that change in the real world has already been effected by the way you are listening to it, simply be-cause keynote listening creates space for listening, and eventually more listeners. And this works in all directions of hierarchy: You don't need to be someone's manager to make them listen. We are talking here about a 3D sphere of change—one in which you influence all around you—those who work for you, your peers, and your bosses, among others.

You, and the listeners you helped create, are not lis-tening for instructions. What you are listening for are gaps. Get friendly with gaps so you can use them.

Optimistic Coda: What Now?

Remember: Gaps are the renewable fuel of new thinking, enabling change. Gaps exploration, around your organization's leading values and ideas, is a great sustainable energy source. By "your organization" I mean your place of work, but also your family and your country. This approach is fully scalable, from intimate relationships to society at large.

How does one go about exploring gaps? By choosing to be ignorant, and by listening from the unique perspective of ignorance. Remember: Ignorance alone will enable you to hear new things people may say, while keynote listening is your tool to help people reach deep into themselves and create new thoughts.

So make ignorance, gaps, and listening into your private code that you can use to enter a desired state of mind, as if you were entering a quiet, luminous space, inviting new thoughts.

Then imagine you have this beautiful gallery of images in your head. One of the rooms of your mental gallery has the images of the six conductors on its walls, inviting you to a stroll—not as a hurried visitor, but rather as an owner: These images are now yours. Look at them to remind yourself of your own path, and where you want to be. Use them as references when you want to understand a piece of your own reality. They are there not to be admired, but to be used. Use these icons as you use this book:

to look through rather than to look at. Everything you'll learn this way will be forever yours, to share and give away for others to look through and discover their own new worlds. You may never know what these new worlds are made of, but you should still realize that they owe their being to your leadership. That should make you, I hope, one very proud ignorant maestro.

ACKNOWLEDGMENTS

I am grateful to my parents, Moshe and Ruth Talgam, whose life stories are a continuous source of inspiration for me. Both my parents are, in many ways, present in this book.

I thank Yuval Ben-Ozer, a fellow conductor and an old friend, with whom I first explored the idea of looking at conducting as leadership, which has developed into my current work. I thank Rina Talgam for her great support during the uncertain times of my professional shift that led to this book.

ACKNOWLEDGMENTS

I thank my literary agent, Lisa DiMona, who was brave enough to improvise a book proposal with me, sitting in a hotel lobby, and also introduced the second LB into my life, the first having been my mentor, Leonard Bernstein. Lary Bloom was about to become very meaningful to me during this new experience of writing. I thank him dearly for that. Moreover, he and his wife, Suzanne Levine, have become, through our daily Skyping at odd times and attires, a much-beloved part of our family. Next in line for my true gratitude is my editor, Maria Gagliano, who did a masterful job in calling to order—intellectually speaking— two unruly old men, LB and myself, always challenging us to do better when we thought understanding our text was someone else's problem.

Many other people contributed to the book: First and foremost all those interested and opinionated people who shared thoughts with me in hundreds of lectures and seminars around the globe. Some, like Francesco Pagano, also shared their thoughts with us in later interviews for the book. Stephen Davis, associate director of corporate governance at the Harvard Law School, offered valuable advice and ideas. Jon Joslow, who in his work as a leader in business has overseen the turnaround of many companies, proved a trusted adviser on this project.

It is a pleasure to mention Simon Sinek for his generosity in bringing my work to the attention of his—now also my—publisher, Adrian Zackheim of Portfolio Penguin. I am grateful to Adrian for his valuable thoughts concerning the manuscript.

I am deeply grateful to my wife, Carianne Vermaak, for sustaining and supporting me in every way, intellectually and emotionally, through the challenges of writing this book. Her wise advice transformed many intimidating gaps into happy insights, and her smiles while reading a new chapter made the effort of writing insignificant.

LARY BLOOM

This book was written in partnership with Lary Bloom.

At first, Lary created a relationship with me. Into it he brought listening and trust in endless supply. For a year or so we were bouncing ideas and stories off each other. We laughed a lot. Our dialogue widened and deepened to encompass unresolved life issues, dilemmas that needed no judgment, only observation and conversation. In the language of this book, we became a team of gap explorers.

ACKNOWLEDGMENTS

One of the gaps most relevant to our work was that between LB's huge literary experience as a writer and editor and my novice's struggle with writing. In a beautiful way, instead of writing for me, LB made me write better. Musically speaking, instead of singing my part with me, he cleverly improvised a second voice, one that made me listen in a fresh way, and get my part better, my voice clearer.

Lary did not always know where we were going (neither did I), but he was listening in a way that could recognize insight, and he knew how to crystallize those insights for the reader. In that important sense, Lary Bloom was the ignorant maestro behind the book, and I was his lucky pupil.

NOTES

PART TWO. THREE NEW THEMES OF LEADERSHIP

CHAPTER ONE. A BRILLIANT IGNORANCE

30 **"they have seen"**: Jacques Rancière, *The Ignorant Schoolmaster* (Redwood City, CA: Stanford University Press, 1991).

CHAPTER TWO. DON'T MIND THE GAP

41 **"where the art resides"**: From transcripts of the twelve lectures by Artur Schnabel at the University of Chicago in 1945 (Hofheim, Germany: Wolke Verlag, 2009); completely revised edition of *My Life and Music*.

NOTES

49 **"a legitimate part of the discipline"**: Conversation with Yair Garbuz, 2012.

CHAPTER THREE. KEYNOTE LISTENING

70 **he famously said:** Nelson Mandela, *The Long Walk to Freedom* (New York: Little, Brown, 1995).

PART THREE. SIX MUSICAL VARIATIONS ON THE THEMES OF LEADERSHIP

74 **"the ruler of the world"**: Elias Canetti, *Crowds and Power*, translated by Carol Stewart (New York: Farrar, Straus & Giroux, 1984).

74 **"at the same volume"**: Kurt Mazur, interview, Mezzo Channel, 1990.

CHAPTER FOUR. COMMAND AND CONTROL: RICCARDO MUTI

88 **"an island of solitude"**: Norman Lebrecht, *The Maestro Myth* (London: Simon & Schuster, 1992).

101 **"with Muti: his way"**: Norman Lebrecht, "Toppling the Tyrant at La Scala," www.scena.org/columns /lebrecht/050323-NL-muti.html.

CHAPTER FIVE. THE GODFATHER: ARTURO TOSCANINI

107 **"such a lovely tone"**: Samuel Chotzinoff, *Toscanini: An Intimate Portrait* (New York: Knopf, 1955).

111 **"fights with fellow executives"**: John Taylor, "Books and Business: Zen and the Art of Computing," review of *Accidental Millionaire: The Rise and Fall of Steve Jobs at Apple Computer*, *New York Times*, Oct. 25, 1987.

NOTES

CHAPTER NINE. IN SEARCH OF MEANING: LEONARD BERNSTEIN

186 **"closest thing I know to love itself"**: Leonard Bernstein, interview, *Omnibus*, CBS, Nov. 14, 1955.

202 *"beastly music"*: Igor Stravinsky, *The Rite of Spring*, Schleswig-Holstein Orchestra, Leonard Bernstein. Schleswig-Holstein Music Festival, summer 1987. Videocassette.

204 **"wonder and serenity"**: Tim Page, *The Glenn Gould Reader* (New York: Vintage, 1990).

207 **"celebrate those differences"**: Audre Lorde, *Our Dead Behind Us* (New York: Norton, 1986).